Cambridge Ele

Elements in Lang
edited
Heath R
University of
Jim McKin
University College London

ASSESSMENT FOR LANGUAGE TEACHING

Aek Phakiti
University of Sydney
Constant Leung
King's College London

Shaftesbury Road, Cambridge CB2 8EA, United Kingdom

One Liberty Plaza, 20th Floor, New York, NY 10006, USA

477 Williamstown Road, Port Melbourne, VIC 3207, Australia

314–321, 3rd Floor, Plot 3, Splendor Forum, Jasola District Centre,
New Delhi – 110025, India

103 Penang Road, #05–06/07, Visioncrest Commercial, Singapore 238467

Cambridge University Press is part of Cambridge University Press & Assessment,
a department of the University of Cambridge.

We share the University's mission to contribute to society through the pursuit of
education, learning and research at the highest international levels of excellence.

www.cambridge.org
Information on this title: www.cambridge.org/9781009468152

DOI: 10.1017/9781108934091

When citing this work, please include a reference to the DOI 10.1017/9781108934091

First published 2024

A catalogue record for this publication is available from the British Library.

ISBN 978-1-009-46815-2 Hardback
ISBN 978-1-108-92877-9 Paperback
ISSN 2632-4415 (online)
ISSN 2632-4407 (print)

Assessment for Language Teaching

Elements in Language Teaching

DOI: 10.1017/9781108934091
First published online: March 2024

Aek Phakiti
University of Sydney

Constant Leung
King's College London

Author for correspondence: Aek Phakiti, aek.phakiti@sydney.edu.au

Abstract: This Element reviews the key foundational concepts, beliefs, and practices underpinning approaches to assessment in English language teaching. Exploring major concepts and practices through educational, social, and ethical perspectives, it offers theoretically informed and close-to-practice descriptions and up-to-date explanations of the affordances and limitations of different assessment approaches related to language teaching. This Element presents a cohesive and pragmatic framework that allows teachers to efficiently implement tests and assessments in their contexts.

This Element also has a video abstract: www.cambridge.org/ELAT_Phakiti

Keywords: language testing, language assessment, language assessment literacy, classroom assessment, English language teaching

ISBNs: 9781009468152 (HB), 9781108928779 (PB), 9781108934091 (OC)
ISSNs: 2632-4415 (online), 2632-4407 (print)

Contents

1 Introduction

This Element focusses on the various forms and practices of language assessment frequently found in educational settings. We will use 'assessment' as a superordinate term and 'testing' where we refer to it as a specific assessment instrument. Assessment is an everyday classroom activity. Various assessment activities can be placed along a continuum from implicit and informal to explicit and formal. For example, when teachers ask, 'Do you have any questions?' as part of a teaching activity, they are said to be engaging in so-called informal formative assessment, which focusses on assessing student learning processes. When teachers evaluate students' submitted work using a scoring rubric and comment on strong and weak points about their work, they are said to engage in formative assessment (FA) if they provide feedback designed to improve learning and summative assessment (SA) if they give a mark, grade, or score without feedback comments. Teachers can, of course, do both.

This Element aims to help teachers develop *language assessment literacy* (LAL), which refers to the knowledge, skills, and competencies involved in the principles, roles, and types of assessment; appropriate assessment tasks and/or task designs; and ethical and fairness considerations (Fulcher, 2012; Taylor, 2009). Teachers can use LAL to help them carry out effective, appropriate, and fair assessments. This knowledge will also allow them to recognise inappropriate and unethical assessment practices whenever it occurs.

1.1 Target Readership

This Element is written for teachers working in different language teaching contexts. We acknowledge that, in contemporary education, the view that only language teachers and assessment specialists need to be concerned with language assessment is changing. For example, in content–language integrated learning (CLIL) and English medium instruction (EMI) contexts, the teachers involved are not necessarily language teachers. Content teachers will likely implement some form of language testing and assessment (LTA) with their students as part of their curriculum work. For example, a CLIL, Year 3 maths teacher needs to help students comprehend a maths question such as 'Tyler's mobile service provider charges him at 5 pence per 30 seconds. How much will it cost him if his phone call lasts 6.5 minutes?'. In this mathematics question, some students' success in answering it can be influenced by the target mathematical knowledge and the ability to construct meaning from a long noun phrase. In this CLIL context, academic language is likely to be taught and explained together with mathematical knowledge. Therefore, all teachers involved would benefit from an understanding that students' content and language knowledge can impact their performance.

In this Element, we mainly use 'teacher/s' to refer to our readers and 'students' as individuals studying in a language programme. Because other terms are also used to describe those being tested or assessed (e.g., test-takers, candidates, and applicants) in the educational literature, we may also use them where they are terminologically and/or rhetorically apposite.

1.2 Overview of the Element

There are eight sections in this Element.

- Section 1 (Introduction) presents the concept of language assessment literacy, target readership and overview of this Element.
- Section 2 (Assessment) provides a background description of some key assessment contexts in English language teaching (ELT). The functions and purposes of assessment are discussed.
- Section 3 (Essential Concepts in Assessment) discusses the terminological distinctions and conceptual connections between testing, assessment, and evaluation. In addition, it provides the essential background of LTA as an academic and professional discipline that teachers can draw on for their understanding of assessment practice.
- Section 4 (Types of Language Assessment) explains two main types of assessment (i.e., formative assessment (FA) and summative assessment (SA)). While not intending to polarise them, this distinction is helpful for teachers to grasp some differences and interconnections.
- Section 5 (Key Theoretical and Technical Concepts) presents a set of key concepts in the design and development of language tests and assessments. Topics addressed in this section include constructs, tasks, and test item types, classical test theory (CTT), and errors in assessment.
- Section 6 (Summative Assessment Design: Types and Processes) considers major iterative stages in developing SA tasks: planning, developing, administrating, and using assessment results. This section includes a discussion of test and assessment techniques.
- Section 7 (Quality Aspects in Assessment) discusses essential quality criteria that ensure effective assessment. Criteria discussed include validity, reliability, practicality, ethics, fairness, and impact.
- Section 8 (Further Developments) points to areas for classroom assessment research that are relevant to teachers and recommends additional resources for professional development.

1.3 Special Features

This Element incorporates a call-out box, *Scan Me*, at various places. This call-out box contains a quick-response (QR) code linked to a selected YouTube video (with a URL also provided) relevant to a topic or issue under discussion. The videos provide additional information or perspectives about the issues being discussed. This shift to an audiovisual mode can make learning about assessment more accessible and meaningful. A guided reflection box is also provided at the end of each main section. Underneath these, a Padlet link is provided for readers to post and share their thoughts with others working in different parts of the world. The authors will engage with the readers' comments and opinions as appropriate. In the final part of this Element, a Glossary of key terms in language assessment is provided for ease of reference and an Appendix contains example test specifications that teachers can consider if/when they wish to develop an SA.

2 Assessment

Assessment is a broad term that includes various approaches and methods for collecting evidence of learning and performance in language teaching contexts. In language teaching, assessment is used to gather evidence of students' language knowledge, ability, skills, and attainment levels for decision-making purposes. Such decisions relate to certification, placement, selection for summative purposes, feedback on learning, and syllabus/curriculum development for formative purposes. Assessment subsumes testing and measurement for eliciting information of interest in a standardised manner (e.g., achievement or language proficiency tests and questionnaires on learning strategies, motivation, or anxiety).

For clarity and practicality, we use 'assessment' as a superordinate term for all assessment activities and 'testing' when we refer to a test for assessment purposes. Generally, testing uses a standardised procedure for collecting student performance information. For example, tests are often administered under strictly controlled time limits and in an invigilated environment (e.g., midterm and final tests, language proficiency tests). It is essential to note that, in the classroom context, assessment can involve activities other than tests, for example a reading comprehension activity, and some tests are used independently of the classroom, for example a commercially marketed test such as TOEFL (Test of English as a Foreign Language) or IELTS (International English Language Testing System).

Two primary stakeholders directly involved in classroom assessment are teachers and students. In language teaching, assessment occurs when teachers ask informal questions during teaching and learning activities, especially if the intention is to check understanding or elicit language production. Students can also monitor and evaluate their learning and that of others during classroom activities or responses to assigned tasks. Teachers can use standardised tests, quizzes, and other assessment tasks, such as project-based, task-based, and portfolio assessments, to promote learning and performance. They may ask students to undertake these activities and tasks individually, in pairs, or in groups.

2.1 Power and Influences of Assessment

All assessment activities have power and consequences (see, e.g., Fulcher & Harding, 2022; Kunnan, 2018; Shohamy, 2001). Sometimes their influence can be subtle and non-directly observable; at other times they can be profound and immediate. For example, when teachers use informal or embedded classroom assessments (e.g., checking student understanding by asking confirmation, clarification, or comprehension questions), they can be said to engage in subtle and non-directly observable but powerful assessment for pedagogic purposes. Teachers can help students improve their learning after observing their answers by providing immediate feedback to their students and modifying their subsequent teaching activities. While such teacher formative assessment practice is implicitly embedded in the ongoing classroom activities, it can have a powerful impact on the quality of learning. With FA, students can learn to independently assess their understanding, gain confidence in their ability to use the target language, and sustain their motivation to learn.

The impact and power of summative assessment (SA) can be more immediate and noticeable, such as when students are asked to take the midterm and final examinations and complete assigned coursework (e.g., individual, paired, or group tasks) that are used to represent their overall achievement in the course (e.g., final scores and grades to be recorded in academic transcripts). The power of such assessment is immediately apparent to both teachers and students. The assessment outcomes can determine students' future opportunities. For example, if students fail a mandatory assessment task, they cannot move on to the next level or stage of their study. They have to repeat the same course. It also means that they will be behind their peers in terms of study completion, and they can lose their confidence, self-esteem, motivation to study harder, and so on.

Scan Me 1

Formative assessment, Walford Anglican School for Girls, Australian Education Research Organisation
https://bit.ly/46M8uAg

The power of external assessment (e.g., college or university admission tests, state or government tests) can impact classroom teaching and learning situations. Students may be required to take a college entrance examination at the end of secondary education. Teachers are often tasked to help students prepare for such an examination. This situation can shift teachers' and students' attention away from the curriculum content (i.e., they gear their teaching and learning specifically to the test). Teachers may get promoted or rewarded if the students' success rate for admission is high. Another example of the power of external assessment is a standards-based assessment of students' literacies and progression by governments and education agencies. Such assessment regimes enable governments to use assessment data to enforce or introduce some academic curriculums nationally and impose assessment outcomes–driven funding models that can directly impact schools, educational sectors, and society.

Globally speaking, governments often devise national educational policies and promulgate standards or benchmarks and curriculums that need to be followed by educational institutions. They rely on standardised testing and assessment to adjudge students' educational standards and attainment levels nationally. Large-scale standardised testing is often deployed to ascertain student learning attainment at a state, provincial, or national level. One underlying, often hidden reason for using standardised assessment by governments is a perceived lack of rigour and trust in teacher- or school-based assessment by external government agencies. For this reason, there is a need to help teachers understand the roles and practices of assessment to change such negative perceptions of their professional knowledge and skills.

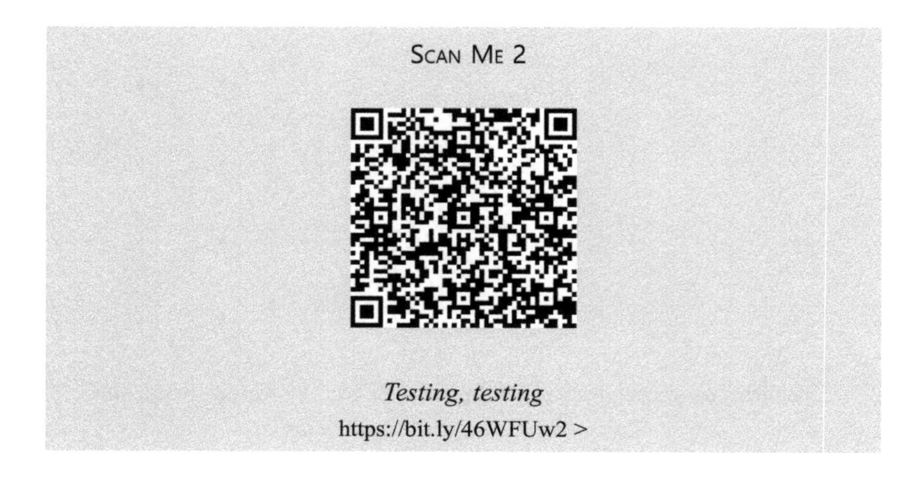

SCAN ME 2

Testing, testing
https://bit.ly/46WFUw2 >

Education systems can enhance their assessment frameworks by providing supportive resources and professional development for teachers so that the educational value of teacher assessment can be positively promoted. With a more positive public perception of teachers' ability to conduct a sound assessment, governments will be more willing to adopt a combination of standardised and teacher-led assessments for evaluating students. This approach is growing in popularity in some educational jurisdictions. For example, in New South Wales, Australia, 50 per cent of school students' achievement is determined by school-based assessment (e.g., teacher and curriculum assessment) and the other 50 per cent by formal state-based examinations. Furthermore, there has been some strong resistance by various state governments to the Australian federal government's attempt to mandate the same national tests for all Australian states. Another example is the Hong Kong Diploma of Secondary Education (HKDSE) English language examination which has a teacher assessment component.

2.2 Assessment in Education

Approaches and practices of assessment vary across language classrooms, educational contexts, and countries. For instance, SA is mandated or implemented, for instance, by official policies (e.g., all students must take part in the national examination program), entrance requirements (e.g., all students must pass the final examination to be eligible for the next course), or authorities (e.g., applicants need to obtain an overall IELTS Band 7 to be eligible for student visas). Standardised tests are often adopted to evaluate students according to established criteria, such as classroom learning outcomes stipulated by state or provincial educational curriculums. Standardised tests are carried out in accordance with strict administrative conditions and are marked or evaluated in the same way for all students; as such, they are seen to be fair because all students are treated in the same way, allowing comparisons among students' performances. On the strength of this reasoning, decisions on students' achievement levels, represented by marks or grades, can often be based solely on their test performances. While standardised tests can be valuable and transparent for decision-making on students, teachers know that the content of many tests does not require their students to perform tasks related to their actual classroom activities or real-life situations.

We note that in anglophone applied linguistics and assessment of English as a foreign/second language, there is a tendency to see the notion of 'stakes' (high versus low) in terms of impact on the individual or institutional functions. The concept of high-stakes within this purview can vary in degree and consequences. For instance, the impact of passing or failing a high-stakes exit or national test in English is first and foremost felt by the student. At the same time, such a test serves an important institutional function for educational institutions (e.g., student selection), employers (e.g., personnel selection of qualified professionals), and society (e.g., fairness for all). Seen in this light, high or low stakes relate to how assessment use affects individuals and society.

SCAN ME 3

What is high-stakes testing – and why hasn't it worked?
https://bit.ly/3RiXMLI>

Classroom assessment focusses on activities in the classroom, which can be *informal* and embedded in teaching and learning activities. Teachers can employ various assessment activities to ascertain student learning and support effective teaching. Teacher assessment can be a dynamic or impromptu reaction to a given teaching–learning situation (e.g., teachers ask students to explain the target grammar rule after they have completed an exercise together). Follow-on activities such as this can reinforce learning. Teachers can also provide feedback comments on students' responses in informal assessment to support further learning. Informal assessment, such as a teacher-led question-and-answer activity, may not immediately impact the student (e.g., passing or failing a mandatory public examination or test, as discussed already). For this reason, informal assessment is sometimes seen as *low-stakes*. If the purpose of assessment is to find out what has been learnt and how to improve learning further, then such informal assessment should not be seen as low-stakes because it is pivotal to the central purpose of education.

Assessments in education vary in the degree of stakes, and they can have different roles in teaching, learning, and decision-making, depending on whether they are immediately impactful or have delayed effects on students and society. A conventionally accepted view that teacher-led classroom assessment is generally low-stakes has been questioned. There is a case to suggest that the use of teacher assessment to enhance learning is educationally high-stakes (see Black and Wiliam, 1998, 2009, 2018; James, 2006; Leung, 2014; Lewkowicz and Leung, 2021; Stobart, 2006).

This Element presents and discusses other formal non-test tasks for evaluating students' learning (e.g., assigned coursework, project-based assessment, portfolios). These forms of classroom assessment have gained acceptability in recent years because they can fully capture students' overall learning and development across time points. The use of high or low diverse assessment frameworks and practices in different contexts suggests a more fluid educational view of assessment impact than the narrower view of high or low stakes traditionally associated with language assessments in English as a foreign/second language contexts. The movement towards balanced types of assessment suggests that teachers need to develop and use a range of learning-oriented and standardised assessments in their educational context.

2.3 Purposes and Functions of Assessment

We have thus far provided a broad account of assessment in language education. We will now look at some major functions that language assessment can serve.

1. Formative function – to enable students to achieve or attain the target learning objectives. The verb 'enable' suggests that the focus of FA or assessment for learning (AfL) is on supporting the achievement of learning targets. When conducting FA, language teachers devise or use various assessment and learning activities to help students develop their knowledge and skills relevant to the learning outcomes. Thus, FA informs teaching and learning. It is designed to help students overcome difficulties (e.g., when they cannot recognise their mistakes, errors, or problems on their own). Teachers' feedback and guidance can help them develop further learning and problem-solving skills or promote positive attitudes towards learning and self-regulation.

2. Summative function – to assess learning achievement or attainment levels at the end of a learning period, whether it is a lesson, a term, or a course. This kind of assessment includes achievement tests, end-of-year examinations, and a class quiz led by the teacher (to check what has been learnt in the lesson). Periodic quizzes may also check student achievement or attainment level as students progress through various lessons. Results of SA can be used to decide whether, how much, or how well students can use the language according to the learning objectives and/or formatively to determine whether students have learnt the specified syllabus content and how best to support their further learning to ensure that they have fulfilled the learning outcomes. Grades or final scores derived from SA can be considered quantitative information indicating students' attainment or mastery relative to the target learning outcomes (discussed further in Section 4).
3. Diagnostic function – to diagnose students' readiness or preparedness. Diagnostic language assessment identifies students' or individuals' strengths and weaknesses regarding specified language abilities or skills. There are various ways in which diagnostic assessments are used. For instance, students can take a diagnostic language test that is relevant to what they will be studying. If the course is related to writing, error detection tasks (e.g., identifying errors in a sentence) may be used to determine whether students can notice grammatical errors. If the diagnostic assessment outcomes suggest they cannot, teachers can use the information to plan further learning support. The DELNA (Diagnostic English Language Needs Assessment) is an example of using assessment for diagnostic purposes for English as a second language (ESL) international students.
4. Placement function – to place students in an appropriate programme or course. The outcomes of an assessment of language proficiency and/or ability can be used to assign students to an approrpiate class or programme. Such assessment often takes the form of a placement test. For example, it will be challenging for students with a beginner's proficiency level to be placed in a more advanced language class that requires advanced reading. Therefore, knowing whether a student's current language ability and skills are suitable for a given class is essential.
5. Gatekeeping function – to admit student applicants into an academic or professional training programme. Admission or selection tests serve gatekeeping purposes. Usually, there are student quotas for an academic or training programme. Therefore, applicants' scores may be rank-ordered before selection or admission. University and college entrance examinations are examples of admission tests (e.g., the National College Entrance Examination (NCEE) or China's Gaokao).

SCAN ME 4

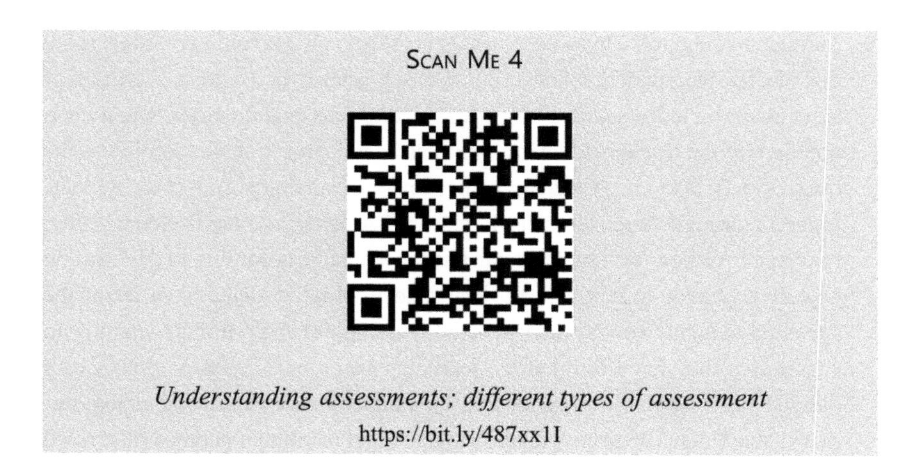

Understanding assessments; different types of assessment
https://bit.ly/487xx1I

Reflection Box 1

Is language assessment necessary for language teaching and learning? Why or why not?

Share your thoughts here: https://bit.ly/3tcbeZX.

3 Essential Concepts in Assessment

This section addresses two aspects of the background of assessment. The first concerns the interconnections among the technical terms testing, measurement, assessment, evaluation, and utilisation. The second is related to the theoretical background of LTA. This section provides a summary account of the background research related to the concept of language proficiency.

3.1 Testing, Assessment, and Evaluation

The discussion of language assessment involves various related terms such as testing, assessment, and evaluation. These terms are associated with both FA and SA. Figure 1 presents the overlapping natures of testing, assessment, measurement, evaluation, and utilisation. This graphic representation suggests a set of complex and embedded concepts in language assessment in educational settings.

3.1.1 Testing

A good deal of educational and professional language assessment is conducted through tests. For this reason, we will refer to testing as a point of departure here and describe the general design characteristics of a language test in ELT. Testing is the first level of collecting information about students or test-takers. It

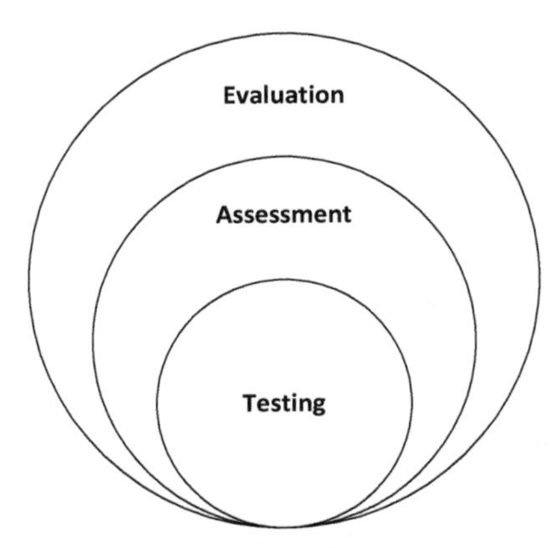

Figure 1 The complex and embedded concepts testing, assessment, and evaluation

involves measurement and is a particular approach to assessment, represented by the larger enveloping circle. Testing includes methods and techniques for eliciting language use or responses to test questions (also known as 'test items' and 'test tasks'). A language test typically includes instructions for students, test questions, items or tasks, or stimuli such as written or audio texts and visuals, and required responses. For instance, students' answers or responses are scored or judged for correctness or appropriateness. Standardised testing requires a predetermined and uniform procedure for collecting language use or responses, and scoring and interpreting performance.

3.1.2 Assessment

As discussed in Section 1, assessment is a concept broader than testing. The primary interest in assessment is to gather evidence for decision-making. Evidence can derive from tests, other sampling tools, and formal and informal observations. Figure 1 suggests that not all assessment activities result in scores derived from testing. Other assessment methods or techniques can yield *qualitative information* that describes the nature of language learning, understanding, or knowledge in terms of accuracy, fluency, complexity, or appropriacy. For instance, in a classroom context, teachers can ask students to explain a concept or idea to find out whether their understanding is correct; teachers can ask students to provide reasons(s) for choosing a particular answer to a test question. In practice, assessments can be conducted in various forms and formats, such as tests, examinations, quizzes, portfolios, and assignments and serve multiple purposes.

3.1.3 Evaluation

Figure 1 shows that testing and assessment implicate evaluation – a process of judging the value or quality of information collected by tests, measures, or other assessment tasks. Evaluation is a broader concept than assessment (depicted in another larger circle). Evaluation requires language teachers to take a broader view of assessment outcomes and to interpret them with reference to other relevant issues. That is, it may require some logical inferencing and reasoning processes. For instance, teachers ask what scores or observed performance mean to students' learning status.

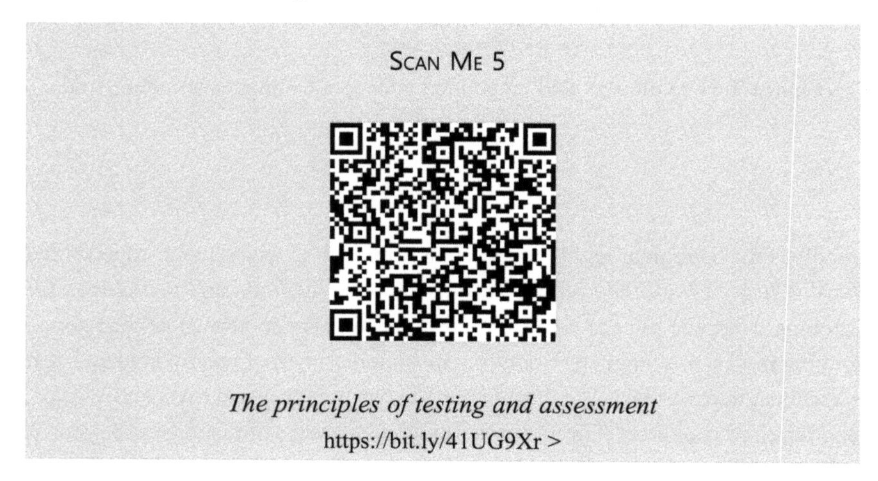

The principles of testing and assessment
https://bit.ly/41UG9Xr >

3.2 Language Ability and Assessment

In this section, we discuss the development of a theoretical framework informing an understanding of general language proficiency. Assessment has been used as a tool for social, educational, and political power and control (see Spolsky, 1995, 2017; Kunnan, 2018, who provide a review of the history of language assessment). For instance, the Imperial Civil Service Examination in China is considered the first examination in the world to produce an administrative elite for governance, dating back to the Sui dynasty, 581–618 CE (Kunnan, 2018). The establishment of this prestigious public examination is a very good example of how assessment can be built into the fabric of the sociopolitical affairs of a society.

In the anglophone academy, the book *Language Testing* by Lado (1961) took a primarily structural view of language in which underlying linguistic systems and rules such as vocabulary and grammar are considered significant in effective language communication; thus, it formed a crucial part of language testing.

Lado's (1961) book was a milestone in testing and language assessment because it helped formalise language testing as a discipline within applied linguistics (see Read, 2015; Spolsky, 1995). In the past forty years or so, the communicative model of language has been prominent (see Section 2.2.1). Further, LTA research in the English language has made invaluable contributions to many aspects of language education (e.g., Fulcher & Harding, 2022; Winke & Brunfaut, 2021). The following subsections discuss the related theoretical concepts influencing our understanding of language proficiency.

3.2.1 General Language Proficiency

Researchers and scholars of LTA have long been developing a theoretical concept of language proficiency that can explain what and how people know and use language across various contexts and situations (see Bachman & Palmer, 2010; Jeon & In'nami, 2022; McNamara, 1996). Language proficiency is a general language ability independent of specific classroom learning or teaching. It may reflect accumulative knowledge and skills acquired through classroom and informal learning. Language proficiency tests assess what individuals can do with a particular language without referencing a specific language syllabus. Language proficiency can be divided into levels, for example beginner, pre-intermediate, intermediate, and advanced. Students at different levels can be described in terms of what they can do with language and how well they can or cannot do it. It is important to know that language proficiency tests are traditionally psychometrically oriented and standardised.

Until the 1960s, LTA was based on a theory that language use behaviours were underlined by human mental structures manifested through the linguistic system, which at the time was understood to be related to lexico-grammatical features (e.g., vocabulary and grammatical knowledge). Hence, language assessment research at the time developed and used test techniques such as multiple-choice, cloze, and short-answer formats for assessing lexico-grammatical features of the linguistic system (see Leung, 2022b; McNamara, 1996; Purpura, 1999).

That said, research in the 1970s onwards started to suggest that language proficiency was multi-componential in that it was made up of more than lexico-grammatical knowledge (see Bachman, 1990; Bachman & Palmer, 1996, 2010; Canale, 1983; Canale & Swain, 1980; Jeon & In'nami, 2022; Savignon, 1972, 1983). Figure 2 provides a sociocognitive model of language proficiency (adapted from Bachman & Palmer, 2010), encompassing cognitive and social dimensions.

The model suggests that various internal linguistic processes interact in language use or learning. In Figure 2, areas within the oval represent internal mental processing and correspond with language tasks and settings. Language proficiency comprises *language knowledge* and *strategic competence* (Bachman & Palmer, 2010), both of which have a social dimension.

- Language knowledge is concerned with knowing and understanding the formal rule-governed structure of language regarding grammatical and vocabulary (also referred to as lexis formally), pronunciation, and conventions of language use in context, including a social and cultural dimension (see also Bachman, 1990). Various aspects of language knowledge are highly connected (e.g., 'went' is a lexical item (word) and the grammatical past tense for 'go'). While various linguistic features are conceptually distinctive (e.g., vocabulary versus grammar), they are not easily separated in language use. In the contemporary language assessment literature, a term such as *lexico-grammatical knowledge* is preferred for describing the knowledge of rule-governed structures.

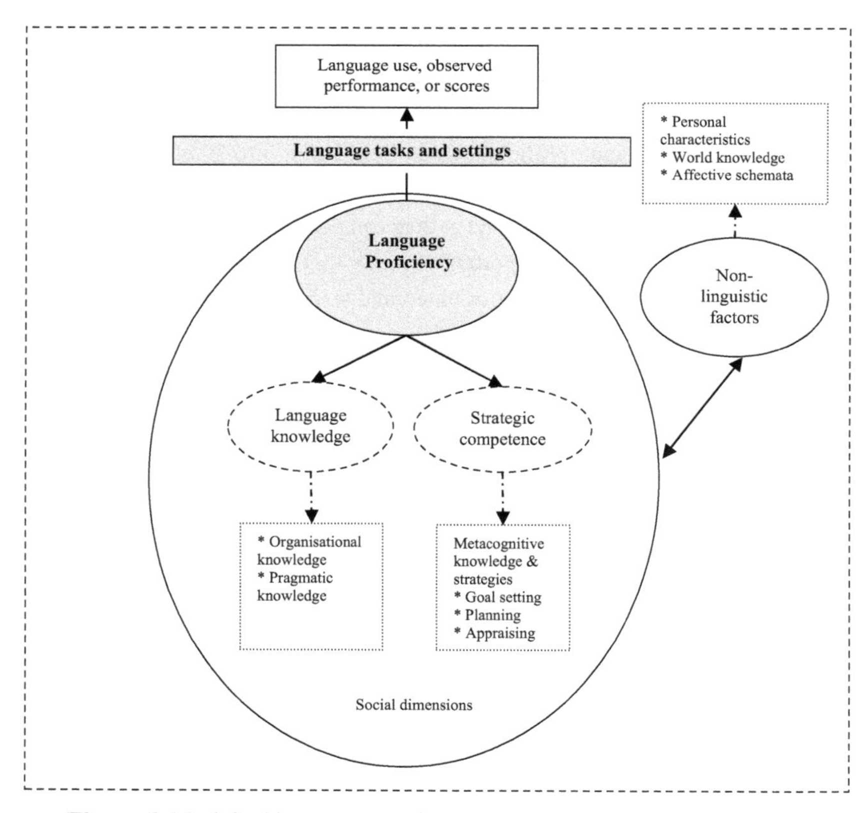

Figure 2 Model of language proficiency (adapted from Bachman and Palmer, 2010)

- Strategic competence is the ability to employ cognitive and metacognitive knowledge and regulation (including practical know how of language use in context), such as working out what things to say and how to say them to best express one's meaning in context (Bachman & Palmer, 2010). Students use various strategies, such as cognitive and metacognitive strategies, to help them process information and complete given tasks (see also Oxford, 2017). According to Bachman and Palmer (2010), strategic competence mediates the language knowledge and non-linguistic factors of a given person, such as personal characteristics, as well as knowledge of the world (or topical knowledge) and affective schemata (e.g., emotions and feelings). In Figure 2, a double-headed arrow links language proficiency to non-linguistic factors. Our current understanding is that strategic competence is not only a cognitive aspect of language use control; it also has a social dimension in that particular ways of thought regulation are shaped by a specific social and cultural context.

In Figure 2, language use, observed performance, and scores at the top of the model are seen as the results of interactions between a given person's language proficiency and the context (i.e., language tasks and settings). This multi-componential view of general language proficiency has had a significant methodological influence on how people's language proficiency is tested or assessed. This view underpins the design of test items requiring students to produce their responses communicatively. This orientation is also reflected by the scoring rubrics in language proficiency tests such as TOEFL and IELTS that focus on assessing test-takers' vocabulary range, pragmatic appropriacy, task fulfilment, and grammatical accuracy.

Scan Me 6

Assessing general language proficiency
https://bit.ly/3TiR1w9

In language assessment practice, it is often necessary to gather evidence of students' specific-purpose language proficiency in a given language within a specific target language use (TLU) domain or situation. Specialist assessment designers can combine features of general proficiency and specific-purpose proficiency to meet the requirements of different disciplines and professions (Douglas, 2000; Moder & Halleck, 2022). An example of a specific-purpose language domain in language teaching is academic writing for engineering. The idea of specific-purpose language proficiency can be useful outside the language classroom. For example, the Occupational English Test (OET) for medical professionals, the Objective Structured Clinical Exam (OSCE), and the Aviation English Language Proficiency Test are specific-purpose language proficiency tests for professional certification and accreditation (see Elder & McNamara, 2016).

3.2.2 Language-Using Skills

Language-using skills typically refer to four distinct modes: listening, speaking, reading, and writing. These are also grouped into *receptive* and *productive* modes. Receptive modes comprise reading and listening skills (decoding and making sense of information), whereas speaking and writing skills are productive modes (encoding and creating information). Language-using skills can be related to general or specific-purpose language proficiency.

Although language use is naturally *multimodal* (meaning that it requires multiple skills or modes to operate or make meaning), in FA and SA situations, test items and assessment tasks are usually designed to elicit performance that can provide information on using a particular language skill. There are also practical reasons to assess one skill at a time: it is easier to design, administer, and interpret results. Nonetheless, a recent trend has been to use *integrated* language tasks that reflect real-life situations, such as in an academic or professional setting (discussed further in Section 4.2.2). We should not automatically assume that all language proficiency tests would cover all four skills equally; much would depend on the purpose of the test concerned.

The following provides an overview of each language-using skill from the perspective of an individual language user.

- Reading skills refer to the ability to process and understand the meaning of written texts (see Alderson, 2000; Brunfaut, 2022; Grabe, 2009). Reading comprehension is derived from the reader's construction and interpretation of meaning from a text through language processing and activation of their prior world knowledge.
- Listening skills refer to processing and understanding audio and spoken texts and obtaining information (see Field, 2008; Rost, 2016). Unlike reading

a written text where the reader can move back and forth, spoken language is temporally streamed, making retrieving what has been missed more difficult.

- Speaking skills refer to the ability to process and produce coherent speech that is meaningful and appropriate for a given purpose in a given context (see Fulcher, 2014; Luoma, 2004). Speaking can be one-way (e.g., reading aloud, talks, announcements) or two-way (e.g., conversations, interviews).
- Writing skills refer to the ability to process and produce ideas or information using a given writing system (e.g., alphabets and letters, word orders, punctuations, syntax) to convey meaning (see Hyland, 2016; Weigle, 2002).

Tables 1 and 2 are examples of language-using skills that underpin constructs in language assessment (see also Brown & Abeywickrama, 2019; Green, 2020; Hughes, 2003). We will focus on linguistic and discourse components for the purpose at hand.

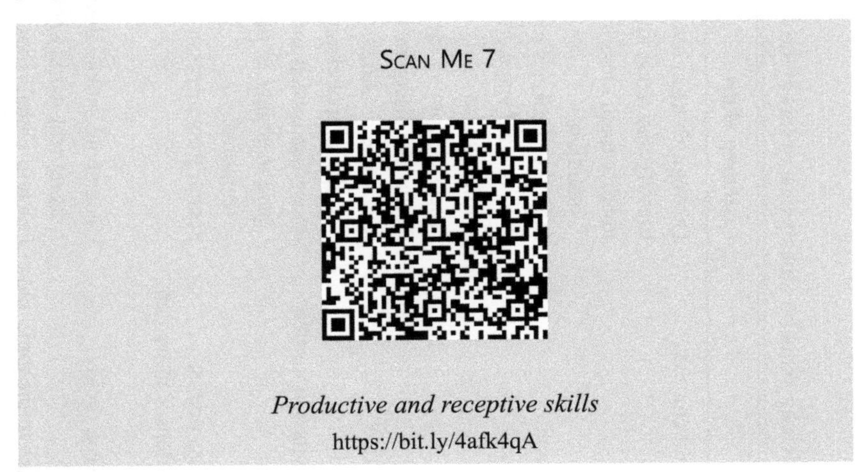

Productive and receptive skills
https://bit.ly/4afk4qA

3.2.3 Language Proficiency Components

It is recognised that language proficiency components and language skills are related. Teachers may need to teach and assess language knowledge or components related to the curriculum tasks in teaching contexts. Therefore, this section presents three language components (grammar, vocabulary, and pronunciation) against which teachers may directly assess their students.

- *Grammar*: Grammar is part of the knowledge of lexical and sentence-level forms and structures associated with a given language. Grammatical knowledge is also connected to pragmatics in that the use of grammar needs to follow expected conventions and to be appropriate, meaningful, and

Table 1 Reading and listening skills (in alphabetical order) of the verbal processes involved

Reading skills	Listening skills
Adjust reading rates to suit a reading purpose and context.	Distinguish main ideas from supporting details or examples.
Identify main ideas and the author's purposes.	Identify and retain specific details.
Infer what writers imply.	Identify main ideas and the speaker's purpose, tone, attitude, or intention.
Predict the content from an introduction paragraph.	Infer the speaker's implied speech or meaning in context.
Recognise spellings and word meanings in context.	Predict what speakers may say next based on the background information.
Recognise types of text and genre.	Process incoming speech at an efficient rate.
Search for and recall specific details.	Recognise discourse markers and cohesive devices in spoken texts.
Skim and scan for general and specific information.	Recognise grammatical functions of words (e.g., nouns, pronouns, verbs, prepositions) and tenses in speech.
Understand discourse markers and cohesive devices in written texts.	Recognise speech sounds (e.g., stressed patterns and reduced forms) and meanings in utterances, and retain them in working memory temporarily.
Understand grammatical functions of words (e.g., nouns, pronouns, verbs, prepositions) and recognise tenses in written texts.	Search for general or specific information.
Use headings, paragraphs, and enhanced texts (e.g., bold, italicised) to assist reading.	Understand spoken discourse meaning (e.g., monologue, dialogue) using real-world knowledge.
Use prior knowledge and/or experiences to relate to the topic and aid reading comprehension.	Use non-verbal clues and body language to make meaningful interpretations.

Table 2 Speaking and writing skills (in alphabetical order) of the verbal processes involved

Speaking skills	Writing skills
Apply pragmatic knowledge such as speech acts and implicatures, as well as conversation rules and social skills (e.g., politeness, turn-taking, and cross-cultural knowledge).	Apply appropriate writing rhetorical forms and conventions (e.g., form completing and personal, professional, and academic writing).
Connect topics, ideas, or arguments to a given situation or event (e.g., use of signposts, conjunctions, and cohesive devices).	
Differentiate and pronounce individual words or sounds intelligibly.	Construct phrases, clauses, and sentences appropriately based on the grammatical system.
Express meaning and speaking intention clearly for a given audience.	Express meaning and writing aim clearly for a given audience.
Produce correct and intelligible stress patterns and intonation contours.	Spell individual words correctly (i.e., spelling).
Produce fluent (e.g., smooth) and natural-sounding speech.	Use appropriate cohesive devices to enhance textual clarity.
Use cohesive devices (e.g., adverbs and pronouns) appropriately.	Use correct subject–verb agreements, function words, word orders, pronouns, prepositions, articles, and so on.
Use correct subject–verb agreements, function words, word orders, pronouns, prepositions, articles, and so on.	Write at an appropriate pace in context.

acceptable in a given context (see Halliday & Matthiessen, 2004; Larsen-Freeman, 1989; Purpura, 2004).

- *Vocabulary*: Vocabulary is related to knowledge of words and word order in a clause/sentence, including formulaic expressions and collocations, and how to use them across various language modes (e.g. reading and writing) (see Read, 2000).
- *Pronunciation*: Pronunciation is tied to phonology (the sound system) and phonetics (sound articulations). It is the vocal manifestation of vocabulary items, conveying grammatical meaning and the speaker's intention through intonation (see Isaacs & Trofimovich, 2017; Kang & Ginther, 2018; Pennington & Rogerson-Revell, 2019).

3.2.4 Social Dimensions of Language Assessment

There are different layers to the social dimensions of language proficiency and language assessment practice (e.g., McNamara & Roever, 2006; Young, 2022). In terms of language proficiency, an individual's underlying language proficiency does not entirely manifest in observed language performance. People's performance in a test is also affected by the tasks, conditions and social interactions involved (e.g., the choice of tasks decided by test developers, the technology used, the type/s of language used in group discussion).

The social dimension in language assessment within an educational or professional context includes the use of assessment by authorities as a mechanism or system for controlling or regulating people's language learning or language use behaviours and choices. Mandatory or compulsory assessments (e.g., final examinations, exit tests, entrance or admission tests) have a political-cum-social function of controlling and regulating students (see Section 1.3). Immigrants are given a test at a particular proficiency level, such as the Common European Framework of Reference for Languages (CEFR) A2, before being granted a visa or citizenship in some countries (see also Rocca et al., 2018; Shohamy, 2006).

From a teaching point of view, it is useful to know the various social functions of assessment in the different classroom and educational contexts. Assessments can be seen as tools to help teachers ascertain learner progress and the extent to which teaching has been effective. In particular, teachers have the power given by compulsory tests and assessments to decide whether students will pass or fail (in a particular course or programme of study). However, formative classroom assessment practice is not necessarily about power and control: FA can engender a unique social dimension for establishing and maintaining a productive teacher–student relationship. The fostering of such relationships should also take account of the sociocultural environment involved. For instance, teachers working in a Confucian-influenced society in Asia, where teachers are often considered to be students' second parents, may find that conducting FA involves different approaches to student–teacher interactions from those in educational environments where such interpersonal relationships cannot be expected. In summary, discussing the social dimensions of LTA helps teachers become conscious and judicious about using tests and assessments on their students.

3.2.5 Multilingualism and Language Proficiency

Until recently, the concept of language proficiency used in LTA was modelled on what native speakers of a given language could do when they communicated (see McNamara, 1996). Such modelling is based on a *monoglossic* ideology underpinning a language proficiency view that idealises the notion of native-speaker competence as the gold standard for learners of English. It follows that language tests and assessments based on such conceptual assumptions have tended to norm the TLU on that of native speakers.

However, an idealised language proficiency model requires some revisions on some theoretical and methodical grounds. For instance, there are many native-speaker varieties of English (e.g., American, British, Australian, Singaporean, and Indian Englishes). Furthermore, a one-standard approach in multicultural, multilingual, and globalised societies can be problematic in LTA. Especially in a localised context, there can be different models and acceptable norms of language proficiency. Many individuals in ethnolinguistically diverse communities routinely communicate with one another through their multilingual repertoire without regard for idealised native-speaker models. Language communication tends to focus more on comprehensibility than on observance of putative native-speaker norms.

Teachers can benefit from understanding the contemporary notion of fluid/flexible *multilingualism*[1] broadly discussed in language education and applied

[1] The term 'fluid/flexible multilingualism' refers to the use of all linguistic resources for communication. For instance, speakers with a knowledge of English, Japanese, and Spanish may draw on their total linguistic repertoire to communicate with one another without necessarily observing language-specific grammatical conventions. The term 'multilingual' is used to refer to societies that have more than one language community, but some members of each language community may be monolingual. The term 'plurilingualism' is used by the Council of Europe (2020) to refer to the communicative repertoire of speakers with knowledge of several languages. A plurilingual speaker uses all of their linguistic knowledge and skills to enhance communication with others. Plurilingualism moves away from the ideal native-speaker proficiency as the ultimate attainment benchmark; instead, it focusses on speakers who can freely draw on their diverse and unique linguistic and cultural repertoire in their communication. In this Element, we use the term 'multilingualism' as it is more commonly used than plurilingualism at this time, but the term 'plurilingualism' to likely to figure in language education and assessment research in future years (see Leung, 2022a for a detailed discussion).

linguistics. Multilingualism acknowledges the coexistence of different languages within individuals in and across societies. In the contemporary language assessment literature, assessing multilingual constructs has been increasingly considered, but it is challenging to accomplish well (e.g., Chalhoub-Deville, 2019; Schissel et al., 2019). Chalhoub-Deville (2019) acknowledged that multilingual constructs could be more problematic for test designers to assess. For example, how should the different languages used by a speaker in a multilingual social interaction be recognised and scored?

SCAN ME 8

Embracing multilingualism and eradicating linguistic bias
https://bit.ly/3GBSI01

An implication for recognising multilingualism in language teaching is that teachers can appreciate the roles of multilingualism in classroom teaching, learning, and assessment. A traditional focus of language teaching and assessing has been on helping students learn and acquire an idealised native-speaker-like language proficiency (as seen by an emphasis on fluency, accuracy, and appropriacy in using a given language in language teaching curriculums and tests). Although relevant research has shown that teachers' and students' own languages (other than English) are used in teaching and learning activities, assessment of students' achievement still focusses only on their ability to use the target language accurately, fluently, and appropriately. An ideal native-speaker proficiency is inadequate and inappropriate to capture multilinguals' language ability and performance in social interaction (for further discussion, see Leung, 2022a, 2022b).

Reflection Box 2

What are challenges you often face when assessing students' language learning?

Share your thoughts here: https://bit.ly/3ReJOKX..

4 Types of Language Assessment

This section discusses FA and SA in greater detail. Figure 3 provides a diagram that conceptualises these two types of assessment in terms of their differences and interrelationships. It should be noted that Figure 3 is not intended to polarise the two types of assessment in language teaching because they are generally nested within an educational or societal system.

In Figure 3, FA and SA appear at the same level, indicating that, educationally, they are both important, with the levels below showing some examples of assessment practices:

- FA collects evidence of students' learning and engagement to improve learning and teaching. It emphasises the importance of understanding students' current developing knowledge related to the teaching–learning outcomes or specific classroom objectives.
- SA is concerned with gathering evidence of students' performances judged against pre-established learning outcomes, standards, or benchmarks. SA includes tests and examinations administered in controlled or standardised conditions (e.g., amount of time allowance and fixed tasks or questions) and other performance assessment tasks such as submitted reports, assigned coursework, and portfolios.

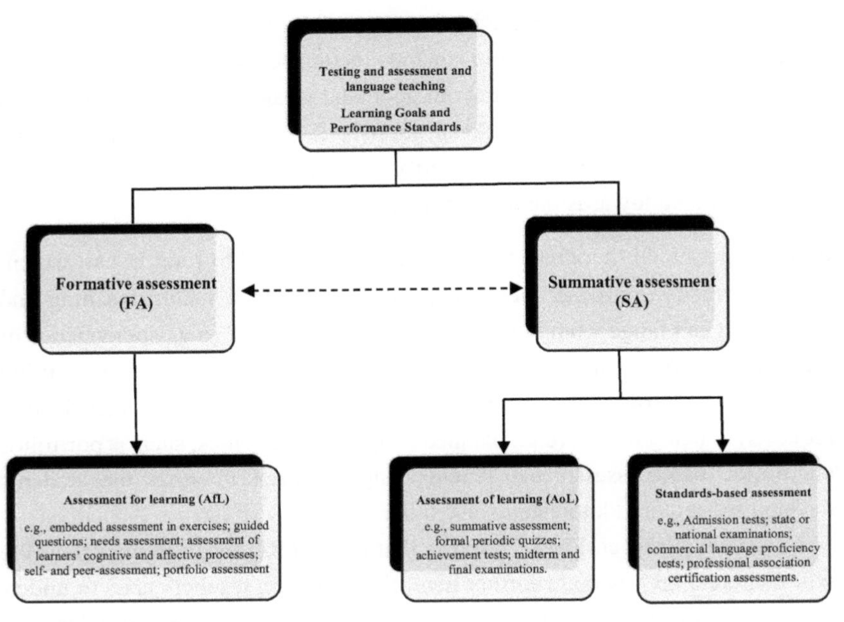

Figure 3 Overview of testing and assessment in language teaching

As shown in Figure 3, FA and SA are interconnected in the classroom ecological network (double-headed arrow). For example, when teachers assess students' understanding of the concept through informal FA (e.g., teacher questioning), they adjudge their students' spoken and written language use against curriculum-derived learning outcomes (which would also inform SA). The expected overall learning outcomes in terms of linguistic fluency, accuracy, or appropriacy inform teacher judgements in FA. An interrelationship between FA and SA is also apparent when summative achievement tests are used for formative purposes. For example, student performances in a midterm test can show the strengths and weaknesses of their current learning progress. This information can be used as feedback, which can help students appreciate what they are already good at and focus on improving their weaknesses. Large-scale external SA (e.g., national or university entrance examinations and internationally marketed language proficiency tests) can influence classroom-based FA and SA practices. The following sections explain Figure 3 in more detail.

4.1 Formative Assessment (FA)

Carrying out FA serves various educational functions and purposes, including:

1. gauging the extent to which students are developing or have developed a body of knowledge and skills or abilities as defined by the target learning outcomes; and
2. observing student learning behaviours to *inform* teaching and learning and using teacher feedback to help students recognise the strengths and gaps in their learning (e.g., by pointing out good and weak aspects of performance) and *feedforward* to help students improve their future performance (e.g., how to avoid similar mistakes or errors in future similar tasks or situations, how to move towards the desired goal).

In the professional literature, the term AfL is also used to refer to assessment with a formative purpose. Generally, AfL is embedded within teaching and learning. It can range from being informal or 'on the run' (e.g., spontaneous or impromptu assessment of students' current knowledge or understanding during classroom activities, such as teachers' use of questions and clarification requests) to being formal (e.g., planned assessment activities, such as portfolios and project-based assessment). Teachers engage in AfL to ensure that students develop the required knowledge and skills.

As indicated earlier, Figure 3 shows that FA and SA are interconnected. We will elaborate on this point further here. For example, teachers need to understand the standards or learning outcomes assessed at the end of a learning period. Such understanding helps teachers observe students' current learning status, thereby enabling teachers to provide helpful feedback and feedforward that will shape students' overall achievement or attainment. Formative insights from in-class SA can yield information for practical teaching plans and material development. We, hence, argue that teachers' SA is directly related to FA in classroom contexts. In language teaching, assessment of learning (AoL) can be teacher-made assessments or tasks and standardised assessments by others (e.g., by the department, school, university, and international testing companies).

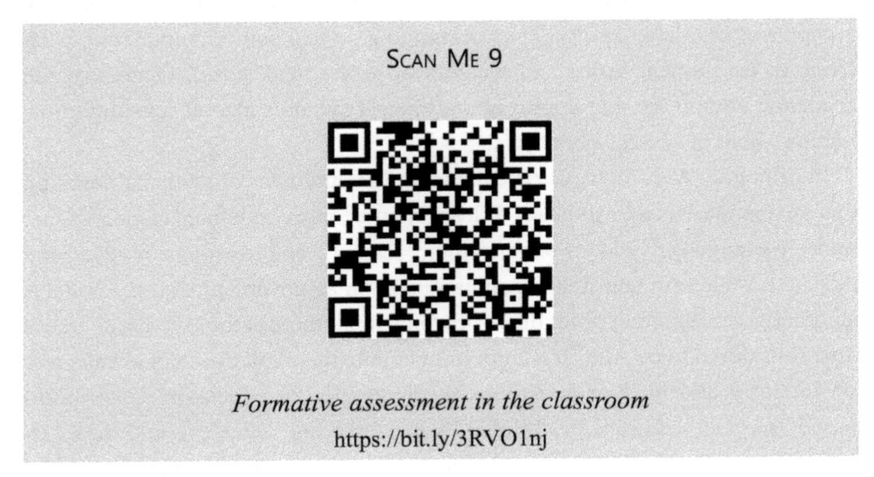

SCAN ME 9

Formative assessment in the classroom
https://bit.ly/3RVO1nj

4.2 Summative Assessment (SA)

Using SA has long been integral to formal education. The term summative implies that assessment focusses on collecting cumulative evidence of students' knowledge, skills, or abilities derived from the teaching and learning activities and engagement at the end of the semester or the teaching and learning period. In a broad sense, SA and AoL are synonymous; they provide accountability for student learning (e.g., grades in academic transcripts and institutional certificates). Official requirements for AoL are also known as *mandates*, which are the frameworks that regulate classroom assessment regimes (Davidson & Lynch, 2002).

Use of SA is associated with a given syllabus's standards or learning outcomes. Standards are the pre-specified criteria of language ability, skills, or learning outcomes that determine what counts as success (or not). Standards-based assessment, such as that provided by the state or by government agencies, is also considered summative. See Brown and Abeywickrama (2019), Harsch and Malone (2021), and Popham (2017) for a detailed discussion of summative and standards-based assessments. Although the boundaries between AoL and standards-based assessment can sometimes be blurry since both involve standards, in practical terms AoL tends to be closely associated with a specific learning point. Standards-based assessments tend to be associated with external mandatory targets or requirements.

4.2.1 Assessment of Learning (AoL)

Traditionally, AoL seeks to determine whether students have met the desired learning objectives of a course. It does not primarily focus on providing feedback for learning or improving learning processes. Typically, AoL is a component of a language syllabus design (e.g., when and how to assess, what kinds of assessment tasks, and weights of assessment tasks). Generally, the academic committee that approves a proposed syllabus also checks the information about the assessment tasks.

In principle, AoL focusses on evaluating the outcomes of students' learning that are compared against the set of learning outcomes or defined standards that underly a language syllabus or curriculum, teaching and learning activities, and AoL (e.g., midterm and final examinations). An achievement test that collects summative information on students' learning attainment at the end of a course is also considered to be AoL. It is important to note that AoL does not always rely on midterm and final examinations in contemporary education. Classroom-based SA can combine traditional (e.g., tests and quizzes) and process-oriented assessments (e.g., take-home tests, assignments, group work, and portfolio submissions). The standards for reading skills for Level 1 on the ESL scales used in Australia for English as an additional language/dialect (EAL/D) learners can be used to exemplify AoL activities:

Standard 1

1. Students can obtain meaning from reading a short, simple text.
2. Students can use basic familiar vocabulary, sounds, and sentence structures to aid their reading comprehension.
3. Students can independently use their classroom reading experiences to complete similar reading tasks and activities.

After AoL data have been evaluated, students are awarded scores or grades that best describe their level of the prescribed standards. In AoL, students' performance should be assessed against the standards (i.e., criteria or benchmarks) rather than being compared with their peers. This approach is called *criterion-referenced approach* (CRA).

Alignment is an important aspect of AoL. Since all forms of assessment can impact student learning quality in various ways, *alignments* among the target

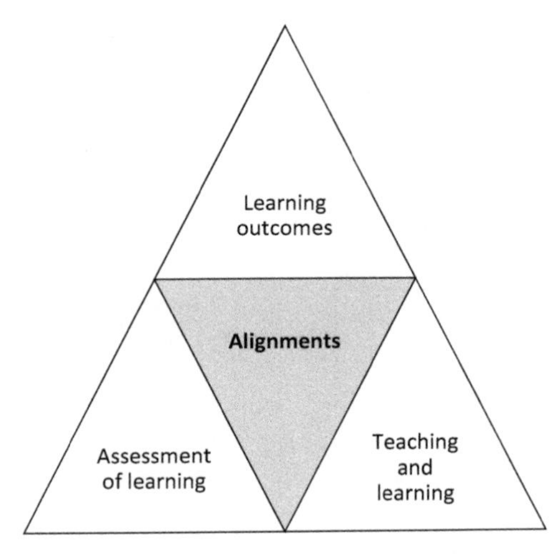

Figure 4 Alignments among learning outcomes, teaching and learning, and AoL

learning outcomes, teaching and learning activities, and assessment are essential. Alignments can warrant assessment relevance and promote fairness in assessment. We illustrate an example of such alignments in Figure 4.

The basics of alignments are that, first, teaching and learning in the classroom should be relevant to the learning outcomes to ensure that students develop their language repertoires in association with the learning outcomes. Second, assessment should be aligned with the learning outcomes and the teaching and learning activities. Figure 5 shows the alignments among learning outcomes, teaching and learning activities, and assessment tasks.

4.2.2 Standards-Based Assessment

A hallmark of large-scale standards-based assessment is standardisation of content and process. In standards-based assessment, the design, administrative, and scoring procedures strictly follow predetermined steps and requirements (e.g., time allowance, proctoring procedures, and scoring methods). It is a procedure that requires all students or test-takers to complete assessment tasks within a strictly observed administrative procedure.

We denote standards-based assessments as those implemented by external agencies or authorities on a system-wide basis, for example a suite of nationwide school leaving examinations. Government standards or benchmarks largely influence school curriculums, syllabuses, and SAs. Influential standards-based tests include *nation- or state-wide standards-based examinations* at statutorily specified times (e.g., by ministries of education). Officially

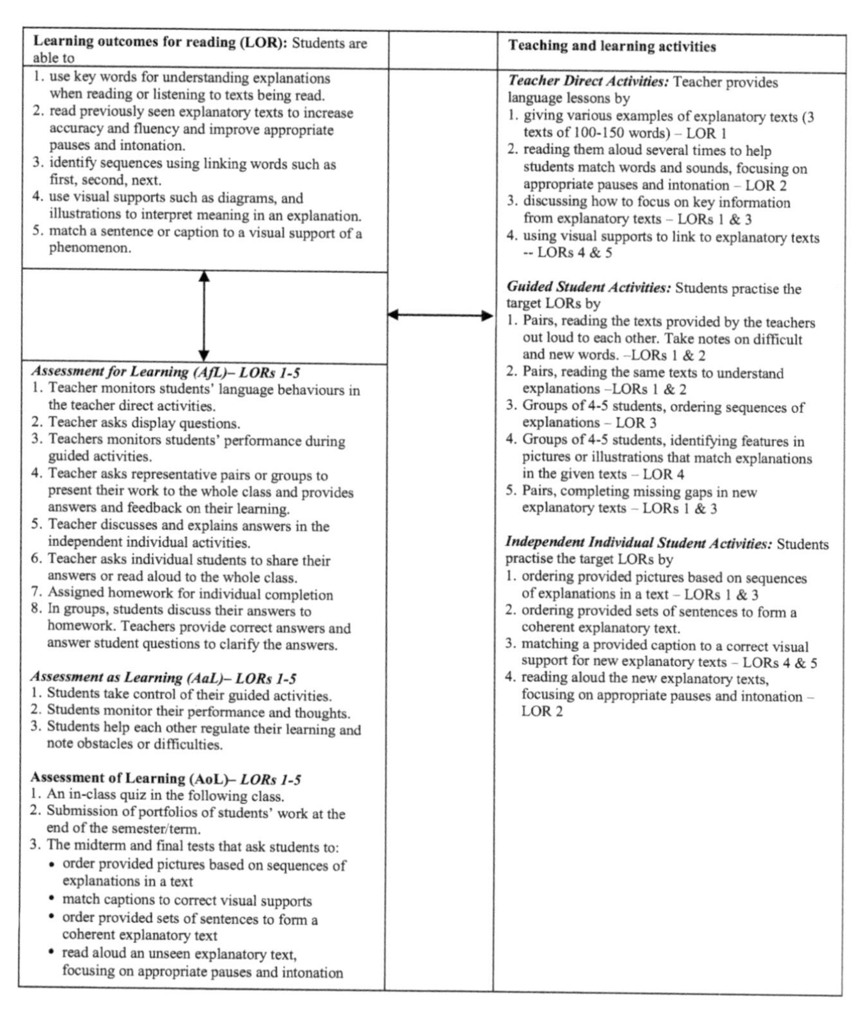

Figure 5 Detailed example of alignments among learning objectives, teaching and learning, and assessment tasks in a pre-intermediate reading unit of study (based on NSW Department of Education and Training, 2004)

mandated standards-based assessments can have government funding implications for schools according to students' performance, and some teachers may be rewarded or penalised depending on students' performance. Governments use such external standards-based assessments to identify, for instance, the level of national literacy and skills required to help determine their country's international economic competitiveness and inform education reform policies.

Other examples of external standards-based frameworks are the American Council on the Teaching of Foreign Languages (ACTFL) Proficiency Guidelines, the Canadian Language Benchmarks (CLB) for ESL, the CEFR, the EAL Assessment Framework for Schools in the UK (published by the Bell Foundation), and the OECD Programme for International Student Assessment (PISA). In Australia, for example, NAPLAN (National Assessment Program – Literacy and Numeracy) is an example of an annual standards-based assessment for Years 3, 5, 7, and 9.

NAPLAN Nightmare
https://bit.ly/41iCIti

Table 3 is an example of an ESL scale in Australia for describing progressions of EAL/D students in different standard phases (e.g., emerging and developing). Table 3 shows some overlapping and transitional content at each competency level.

4.2.3 Types of Decision-Making in SA

We have seen already that SA is used to decide on students' achievement or success levels. Two types of decision-making approach are commonly used in assessment practices: the norm-referenced approach (NRA) and the CRA.

Norm-Referenced Approach (NRA)

The term 'norm' is derived from the normal distribution concept of test scores (bell-shaped distribution; see Figure 6). The normal distribution is a probabilistic frequency distribution of quantitative data or scores in which the average or mean score is used as the midpoint in the distribution (the 50 per cent point). The standard deviation (SD), a statistical measure that estimates the spread of scores in a given sample or population, is used to help establish the distribution curve.

Table 3 Example of the ESL standards (emerging and developing phases) for EAL/D students in Years 3–6 (based on Australian Curriculum, Assessment and Reporting Authority (ACARA), 2014, pp. 9, 16)

Emerging level	Developing level
At the beginning of this phase, students demonstrate the ability to understand simple short texts with varying success. Students are able to: 1. develop linguistic knowledge of predictable English sound–symbol relationships and some common letter patterns 2. recognise common subject-specific words 3. comprehension 4. understand familiar prints around the classroom (e.g., posters and signs) 5. read their own writing correctly 6. read short texts with predictable structures and everyday language 7. read texts out loud, following the print from left to right and top to bottom, using appropriate pauses and intonation 8. understand some gist or main ideas in simple short texts 9. use their current spelling and pronunciation knowledge to attempt pronouncing new words. As they reach the end of this phase, they become more independent in their reading and realise the purpose of reading.	At the beginning of this phase, students demonstrate the ability to understand more complex and longer texts with a good success rate. Students are able to: 1. become more independent in their reading than in the emerging phase 2. when instructed, recognise common suffixes and prefixes, and use these to construct meaning (e.g., -ly for the adverbs of adjectives) 3. identify the gist or the main idea in most class texts correctly, and in more complex and lengthier texts that have predictable structures and contain familiar vocabulary, although they may still depend on some illustrations 4. identify characters in texts 5. search for specific factual information. As they reach the end of this phase, they are able to: 6. recognise various purposes of texts and reading comprehension 7. recall and retell sequences of events or stories accurately 8. make some inferences 9. adjust their reading rate to cope with available time allowance and tasks 10. read aloud most class texts correctly, with confidence and appropriate intonation (e.g., statements, questions, and dialogue).

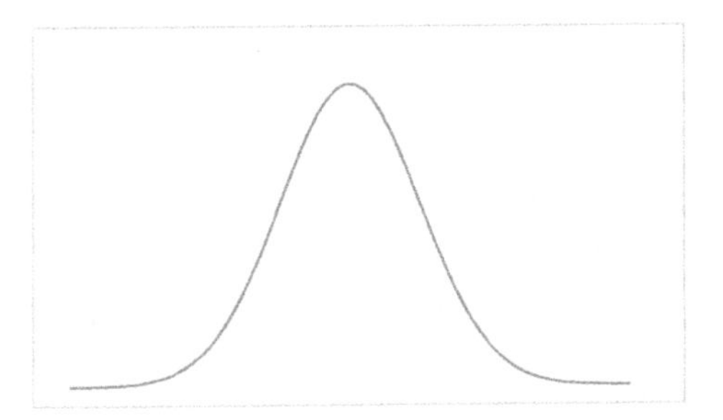

Figure 6 The normal distribution

As illustrated in Figure 6, SDs are placed around the mean (average score). A minus sign appears before them when they are below the mean, but no plus sign is used when they are above the mean. Theoretically, this kind of score distribution suggests a ranking system. For example, students whose scores are below the mean score are considered below the average, whereas those above it are considered above the norm; how far below or above is defined by the values of SDs.

The perfect normal distribution of scores is symmetrical (mirror image) on the left and the right sides of the mean. When the normal distribution is considered, scores are placed along a continuum of the lowest and highest possible score. When there is a normal distribution, many students will likely be placed around the average score (approximately 68 per cent within ±1SD). To illustrate, if the mean score is 60 and the SD is 10, the scores between the mean and 1SD can range from 60 to 70 (making up approximately 34 per cent of all students), and the scores between the mean and –1SD can range from 50 to 60 (also making up around 34 per cent of all students).

However, a perfect normal distribution (i.e., symmetrical) is unlikely in a dataset because the normal distribution is affected by sample size and the heterogeneity of students' abilities (high, medium, and low), among other things. Through the normal distribution principle, NRA adopts a ranking system of students' scores (e.g., the highest to the lowest) for decision-making on students. There are reasons for NRA to be used in many standardised standards-based assessment contexts, for example where students are compared with others in a given school across different states or provinces. The type of decision-making in the NRA is *relative* (see Brown, 2005). Scores are first ordered and calculated in percentiles. In statistics, a percentile of a given student indicates the proportion of students who score above or below them. For example, students with a *percentile* score of 90 perform better than 90 out of 100 but worse than 10 out of 100. In Australia, for example, students who have completed a two-year higher school certificate in most states are given an Australian Tertiary Admissions Rank (ATAR) score. Their grades and subjects are calculated to derive each student's ATAR score, which is out of 100 (i.e., a percentile). Therefore, if a student's ATAR is 95, it means that this student performs better than 95 per cent of the students (i.e., this student is in the top 5 per cent). Generally speaking, a high ATAR is specified for a competitive field of study (e.g., medicine) in a highly ranked university.

In summary, NRA is used in SA when limited places, quotas, or positions are available. It is also used in general or specific-purpose language proficiency tests in which test-takers must be identified as beginners, intermediate, or advanced, and so forth. In practice, even though scores may not be normally distributed, scores are rank-ordered, and those with the highest scores are selected.

Criterion-Referenced Approach (CRA)

An example of a CRA is a driving test. It is of no interest to the licensing authorities whether candidates are the best or the worst drivers among all candidates before they are given a driving license. The driving test officer has the official criteria and must determine whether a given candidate has met each of them (e.g., speed management and vehicle control). In the end, the decision is a yes/no decision. Candidates of a given day are not compared against one another for decision-making.

The driving test scenario can be applied to classroom-based SA. Students' achievement or attainment performances are decided using the given learning outcomes (i.e., criteria). For example, in a reading lesson, if one objective is 'students can identify the main idea in an expository text', and if students can correctly answer the questions related to the main ideas in a reading test, then it can be said that those students have met the objective (i.e., passed). In practice, the cut or minimum expected scores decide whether students have met the criteria or standards (e.g., at least 70 per cent correct). In this example, students' scores are not ranked as in the NRA. Accordingly, CRA focusses on matching or aligning students' performance against the given standards or criteria (see also Fulcher, 2010). In other words, the CRA decision is *absolute* as it focusses on whether a student has achieved the stipulated benchmark, be it in the form of a single answer or a minimum number of acceptable answers/ responses.

Of course, in many language courses, students are not necessarily given a pass or fail grade. There may be different letter grades that are associated with a range of percentage scores (e.g., 0–49 = F, 50–59 = D, 60–69 = C, 70–79 = B, 80–89 = A, and 90–100 = A+). The decision to award particular grades to students would depend on where their scores fall in the ranges. In this grading system, teachers should use percentages (rather than percentiles) to decide students' achievement levels or grades. If all students have scores between 90 and 100, they should all receive A+.

Reflection Box 3

Should assessment for and of learning be norm-referenced? Why or why not?

Share your thoughts here: https://bit.ly/4aaPyhx.

5 Key Theoretical and Technical Concepts

This section elaborates on some methodical concepts that language assessment professionals apply in test or assessment design (e.g., constructs, CTT, and types of error associated with assessment). Some aspects of these concepts are relevant for both SA and FA.

5.1 Constructs in Assessment

Teachers may encounter the word *construct* when they read a test manual or technical report of a given test or assessment. Constructs represent *abstract* concepts of knowledge and skills. *Language proficiency* is an example of a construct because it is abstract. We cannot observe it directly, but we can make it 'knowable' through tests or assessments, allowing inferences and evaluations to be drawn from responses to test questions or tasks. Constructs such as language proficiency or skills are theorised to manifest observed language use or responses to test tasks for inferring the constructs of interest. For example, speaking fluency can be inferred by observing how students talk when they respond to a given task. Reading comprehension can be inferred by observing whether students answer comprehension questions correctly. Assessing what we cannot define is difficult because we do not know what we seek in students' abilities or knowledge. Teachers may not use the term construct, but terms such as language skills and learning outcomes or objectives in their assessment would be part of the established professional terminologies.

Knowing what to assess is important for at least two reasons. The first is related to FA. When teachers employ FA during their teaching, they can be more aware of what they are looking for in their students (e.g., abstract ability, language skills) as they interact with classroom activities. For example, teachers can recognise students' errors or inappropriate language use. Knowing what to assess allows teachers to effectively use their time and effort to gauge and support students' learning. The second implication is related to SA. In AoL, test-writers and teachers can explicitly define what language knowledge or skills they aim to assess in their students. Explicit definitions can provide a checklist for evaluating questions or tasks that students will complete (e.g., quizzes, midterm and final test questions, and tasks for portfolios). By being explicit about what to assess, teachers can check whether their assessment constructs are aligned with classroom tasks and activities. Likewise, test-writers can check the alignment between test design and curriculum and/or syllabus specifications.

Scan Me 11

CEFR and language assessment
https://bit.ly/41cNktX

5.2 Ways to Elicit Performance (as Evidence of Learning/Knowing)

This section elaborates on fundamental considerations when teachers elicit or collect evidence of student learning or performance (as specified in the learning outcomes). Suppose teachers aim to know whether students can orally tell others about themselves (e.g., their names, hobbies, or interests) after a lesson. In that case, they can design a paired task where students exchange information about themselves. This method seems appropriate and relevant. If, however, students are asked to complete missing gaps in a written conversation dialogue, their speaking is not appropriately assessed. In this situation, their performance also depends on reading comprehension and writing skills.

Language assessment professionals have developed and fine-tuned the use of test or assessment techniques for assessing language skills or components (see Brown & Abeywickrama, 2019; Green, 2020; Coombe, 2018; Weir, 1990, 2005; Winke & Brunfaut, 2021). This section considers three (interrelated) methods for eliciting students' performance.

5.2.1 Elicitation Approaches

The three frequently used approaches for eliciting language performance are direct, semi-direct, and indirect. Discussing the extent of directness is useful when considering the level of task engagement and involvement, which require various skills and processes.

1. *A direct approach* asks students to directly engage in the focal language-using skill (e.g., students engage in reading when we assess their reading ability). It is called 'direct' because it is strongly related to the construct of interest. This approach allows teachers to understand how well students can complete skill-specific tasks. A speaking test that asks students to interact with prompts from a computer (e.g., by speaking into a microphone) is an example of a *semi-direct approach*.
2. An *indirect approach* asks students to perform language tasks that involve using a particular piece of language knowledge and/or skills relevant to the target construct (e.g., grammar or vocabulary tests for inferring reading or writing, or pronunciation tests for inferring speaking). The indirect approach does not require students to engage in a full range of requisite language knowledge and language-using skills. For example, *error detection tasks* ask students only to identify an ungrammatical option in a sentence. Although accurately identifying errors in a sentence can be linked to the lexico-grammatical knowledge required for good writing, an error detection task is indirect to assessing writing because it does not ask students to write sentences or essays.

Choosing the most appropriate method to assess language skills (i.e., direct or indirect) is critical because it influences the level of inferences and generalisation. Indirect approaches are not suitable for making holistic claims about students' language use since they have not produced the language independently. For instance, in an indirect speaking task such as a pronunciation test, students may pronounce individual words correctly, but the extent to which their pronunciation is comprehensible in communicative speaking tasks is not fully known.

5.2.2 Integrated Approach

A good deal of language assessment now adopts an integrated approach. There are two related ways of understanding this approach, represented by two related terms – integrative and integrated:

1. Integrative tasks require students to use various aspects of language knowledge and language-use skills to respond to a given question or task. For

example, a *dictation* task that asks students to write what they hear is integrative since it requires them to integrate their listening and writing skills, vocabulary, grammatical knowledge, and spelling skills. Similarly, a *cloze task* that asks students to fill in a gap in a phrase or sentence with one suitable word only requires them to read the text for global comprehension and to use a specific vocabulary and correct syntactic form (i.e., vocabulary and grammatical knowledge) in the provided space. The word integrative, therefore, suggests an interactive nature of language use as students respond to the task.

2. Integrated tasks are considered to be a variety of integrative tasks. Unlike the need to integrate different aspects of students' own language knowledge, skills and processes in dictation or cloze tasks, they are explicitly asked to select and/or use a set of provided stimulus materials (e.g., written or spoken texts) in combination to generate their test performance. For example, students are asked to read a written passage about public health and to listen to a talk on a related topic. Then, they need to speak to respond to a question or prompt by using information from the reading and listening texts to form their viewpoints. In this example, students are said to integrate various sources of information to produce their responses. Integrated tasks are useful for assessing language production directly, such as speaking and writing for a specific purpose. Receptive skills are indirectly evaluated in such an integrated test task.

5.2.3 Selected- or Constructed-Response Techniques

Many teachers are familiar with techniques such as multiple-choice, true/false, and short-answer questions, as well as essay and interview tasks. In the language assessment literature, these techniques can be classified into selected- or constructed-response categories. The term *selected-response* suggests that students must choose from the provided options to respond to questions or tasks. In contrast, the term *constructed-response* indicates that they can produce (i.e., construct) their own answers or responses. Therefore, the multiple-choice and true/false techniques are selected-response, whereas essay and interview tasks are constructed-response techniques.

Knowlwdge about these techniques is helpful for both FA and SA because there are advantages and disadvantages associated with these techniques. Some techniques are regarded as suitable for a particular language use. For example, selected-response techniques are often used to assess receptive skills, whereas constructed-response techniques are often used to assess productive skills.

Therefore, matching a technique to the target construct is crucial for language assessment.

5.3 Classical Test Theory (CTT)

Developed in the early to mid-twentieth century, CTT is related to a body of psychometric theory in ensuring accuracy and reliability in test scores (see Brown, 2022; Sawaki, 2014, for detailed discussion). Brown (2022) argues out that CTT helps teachers understand abstract testing and assessment concepts. Constructs, for instance, are abstract, so it is plausible that errors can occur in an assessment process. Test reliability and error in testing and assessment are well-conceptualised within CTT. In a nutshell, CTT is a measurement theory that focusses on the accuracy and consistency of collecting relevant and sufficient information about an aspect or construct of interest. It aims to connect an observation (e.g., as represented by performance criteria and/or test scores) to an underlying construct of interest.

Brown (2022) argues that it is a misconception that CTT is a *thing of the past* or an *old-fashioned theory* that is no longer relevant to language assessment. He asserts that CTT is still relevant to many practices in language assessment and is widely used, especially in educational and professional settings. He suggests that some may perceive it to be old-fashioned because it has been overshadowed by more sophisticated alternative measurement theories, such as the Item Response Theory (IRT) and the Generalisability Theory (G-theory) used by assessment researchers and test companies (e.g., Educational Testing Services, Pearson Education).

One of CTT's core assumptions is that a test score comprises what we are looking for plus some irrelevant information (labelled as errors) that can interfere with or give a false understanding of students' ability, knowledge, or attainment, for example. We summarise this concept as follows:

A test score = A true score + an error score

According to this principle, the first component of a test score is a *true score* that is explained by what we aim to assess (e.g., the underlying construct(s)) by asking students to complete test tasks or questions. For example, we seek to know whether students can give directions using a map. In that case, their scores should represent their ability to use appropriate words, comprehensible expressions, and specific information relevant to the map. As can be seen from this example, the ability we are interested in includes grammatical and lexical knowledge, pronunciations, social skills (e.g., turn-taking, politeness), and knowledge of how to read a map. This is the part of scores we often think of as a true score – what underlies a given score.

CTT and operationalisation
https://bit.ly/3TUMmRn

Hypothetically, if a score comprises a true score plus zero error (true score + 0 error), a test or assessment has captured 100 per cent of the underlying construct. However, it is unlikely that a test score is made up only of a true score since various interfering factors can impact students' performance. Therefore, in CTT, the products of interfering factors or conditions are known as 'errors' or an 'error score'. Now let us return to the example of the map-reading and giving direction task and think about possible errors that may affect a score. We will use two scenarios to explore plausible errors:

Scenario 1: Jay is generally good at speaking and is familiar with giving directions to places using a map from the classroom activities. She is short-sighted but forgot to bring her glasses to the test room that day. She also had her wisdom tooth removed two days before the test. Consequently, in this test, she could not see the map clearly (as it was also relatively small and in black and white), and she felt uncomfortable when speaking owing to some pain from the dental surgery. She had to guess some street names and places on the map. Jay felt upset and worried during this test because she could not pronounce words intelligibly. Jay subsequently got a low score owing to her poor performance. Is Jay's score an accurate picture of her ability? What could be the errors in this test? What might be a problem with using the current score to decide her speaking ability?

Scenario 2: Mike is an average speaker and happened to know what map was to be used in the test beforehand. Therefore, he memorised street names and places and practised giving various directions based on the map several times. Mike produced an impressive speaking performance with fluency and accuracy in this test. Subsequently, Mike received a top score. Is Mike's score an accurate picture of his ability? What could be the errors in this test? What might be a problem with using the current score to decide his speaking ability?

As can be seen in Scenario 1, some factors other than the target ability influence Jay's performance (e.g., no eyeglasses, a small map, an inability to speak comfortably, and the associated effects they have on Jay, such as causing her to become upset and worried). Because Jay's ability is high, her test score is not representative of her ability and, hence, the observed score contains many errors. In Scenario 2, we do not know how much Mike's score represents his ability because he was familiar with the map used and had memorised what to say. We might know more by asking him to do the task with a map he has never seen and finding out whether he performs similarly well. Nonetheless, we know that his current score cannot represent his ability. Should we construe Mike's background knowledge and familiarity with the test task as an interfering factor contributing to the measurement error?

In CTT, an *error score* is theorised to be contributed by factors other than the construct(s) or aspect(s) of language knowledge and ability of interest. Such known factors include testing or assessment methods, administrative and scoring conditions, and students' factors such as current illness and fatigue (see also Bachman & Palmer, 1996; Brown, 2005 for further discussion). Our hypothetical examples of Jay and Mike suggest that the more the true score is included in an observed score, the more valuable the score can be when it comes to decision-making (Brown, 2014).

The proponents of CTT have developed and used rigorous and robust systems in test design, standardised administration, and scoring to minimise errors. For example, a test should not rely only on one task or question because it cannot adequately sample students' abilities. Therefore, CTT has a tradition of dissecting errors from true scores and improving a test or assessment that can eliminate systematic errors. The development of CTT, no doubt, has led to statistical analyses of test reliability such as internal consistency (with reference to parallel tests and items), item difficulty, discrimination of different ability levels (note the discussion of test discrimination as a test function is not related to racism or sexism), test–retest reliability, split–half reliability, and so on (see Bachman, 2004; Brown, 2005, 2022; Lynch, 2003; Roever & Phakiti, 2018; Sawaki, 2014, 2017 for further details).

To understand CTT, it is also important not to confuse the notion of CTT errors with 'mistakes' that students make in assessment. In FA, teachers benefit from knowing students' mistakes since they can provide corrective feedback and other support to help students correct their errors. Students' mistakes are not the same as measurement errors in assessment (manifested through testing and test scores). For example, when a teacher asks her students to explain the grammar rule related to a communicative task they are learning, one student representative explains it correctly. Therefore, the teacher feels delighted that her students have got the concept right. However, in the exam, most students fail to correctly use the grammar rule in a similar task they had accomplished in the classroom. To the teacher, this is a shocking discovery. In this scenario, the teacher might have made an error in her generalisation about student learning: while the student representative might have correctly understood the grammatical concept, the rest of the class might not have. Therefore, more students with different ability levels should have been asked to avoid such errors. In this example, the teacher's inaccurate understanding creates the illusion of student collective knowing. Such an observation error can be likened to an error score in CTT, leading to ineffective assessment.

Finally, CTT has limitations, for example its reliance on the use of raw scores to estimate errors, its assumption of item equivalence across the whole test (i.e., sum scores), and error of measurement being treated the same for all ability levels.

Understanding CTT is beneficial for teachers when they design a test or assessment task or use an already developed test; it makes them aware that a single observation is likely to result in a misleading conclusion about performance. Awareness of errors in assessment is relevant to tests and other non-test tasks such as portfolios and assigned coursework. For example, in portfolio assessment of young children, parents may assist their children in completing their portfolios. Therefore, the portfolio may include contributions from the parents involved. Furthermore, in another non-test condition, many unknown factors can contribute to errors in assessment. For example, students may use Chat Generative Pre-trained Transformer (ChatGPT) to help them write an essay that can be completed at home, but they cannot access any such assistance when they are asked to hand-write an essay in a controlled testing condition. Their writing scores can differ significantly under these different conditions.

Reflection Box 4

What do you do to reduce errors in FA or SA?

Share your thoughts here: https://bit.ly/3t35TnR.

6 Summative Assessment Design – Types and Processes

Stages in designing a test for summative purposes can differ from those used in non-test administration conditions (e.g., portfolios and task-based assessments, which can combine FA and SA). Non-test classroom assessment can take different forms and involve several stages flexibly to suit the context of a given classroom situation. For example, in a portfolio assessment, students can choose their topics and set their portfolio goals. They have out-of-class time to work on their projects and receive teacher and/or peer feedback as they complete their tasks. The international baccalaureate diploma, for example, has a project-based component for SA. In the Nordic countries, classroom assessments are generally teacher-led, and in general the school systems use only standards-based testing at school leaving age. The following section aims to provide an overview of test and assessment designs that may be relevant for teachers when considering assessment for different purposes.

6.1 Test Design

There can be situations in which teachers need to develop a test (e.g., midterm and final examinations, screening tests, admission tests). In such situations, teachers are assumed to be knowledgeable in creating test tasks or quizzes for their students. Their school or academic institute may ask them to design a test. The following design stages, as illustrated in Figure 7, can be seen as a road map for test development.

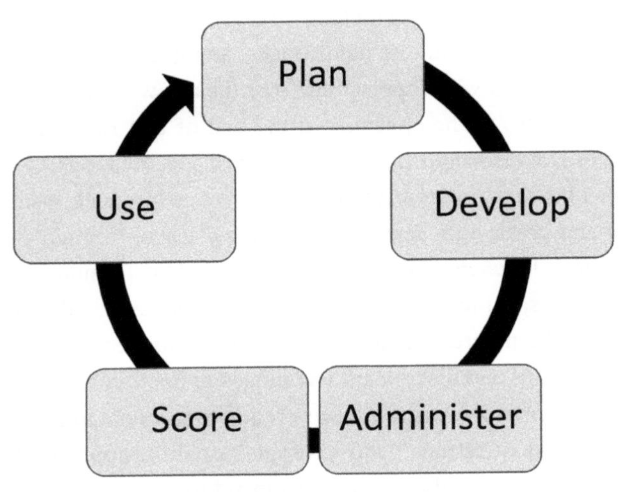

Figure 7 Five stages in test design

6.1.1 Stage 1 (Plan)

Planning is essential in test design because it allows teachers to ask relevant questions, for instance: What are the reasons or purposes of the given test? Who are the target students and relevant stakeholders? What are the constructs or learning outcomes that will be assessed? What techniques (e.g., selected- and constructed-response techniques) will be used? What are the resources required for developing the test task? What is the time frame for completion of the test development?

6.1.2 Stage 2 (Develop)

Since language tests are based on standards that define the target knowledge, abilities or skills, teachers need to engage in the following preparations: developing test specifications, creating questions and tasks, and piloting and improving them before actual use. We note that some of these considerations are also relevant for other non-test assessments, for instance portfolios and assigned coursework.

1. *Test or assessment specifications* (also known as blueprints) provide a detailed outline of the test or assessment structures (see Bachman & Damböck, 2017; Carr, 2011; Davidson & Lynch, 2002 for comprehensive coverage of this topic). A test specification can give an overview of the sections that assess specific language skills. Test or assessment specifications can help guide teachers when they write items or tasks. When evaluating test specifications, teachers should focus on the alignments among the constructs to be tested, the methods and tasks being used to elicit student performance, and the scoring methods. Test specifications can evolve and be improved over time, and test items, tasks, and questions can be collected, revised, and reused when appropriate (see the arrow from 'use' pointing to 'plan' in Figure 7). The appendix at the end of this Element provides an example of Davidson and Lynch's (2002) test specifications.
2. *Question and task creation* requires teachers to produce instructions for students and create test items (questions and tasks) to elicit responses or performance. Teachers need to choose assessment techniques when they develop their specifications. Assessment techniques are determined with reference to the nature of language skills or components. (We will further discuss some test and assessment techniques in Section 5.1.6.)
3. *Piloting and/or improving before use* requires teachers to gather information about test questions' and prompts' quality, appropriateness, and suitability. A pilot study can start from internal team reviews (e.g., all

teacher-cum-test-writers review one another's test tasks or questions, checking for alignments of constructs and assessment tasks, typographical errors, and clarity and appropriacy of tasks, and making suggestions for improvement). It can also involve expert reviews (e.g., getting language testing experts to review whether tasks conform to expectations), to check for language accuracy and authenticity, and trial or pilot testing with some students who are similar to the target group. All of these activities should lead to improvement of the test quality.

After these sub-stages have been completed and the tasks and items have been corrected and improved, the test can be assembled for administration and use (which involves formatting, programming, second-round pre-testing or piloting if needed, deciding on the scoring methods, and ensuring test security such as no accidental release of the test before the scheduled administration).

6.1.3 Stage 3 (Administer)

This stage is concerned with test administration. Test administration refers to the process of managing and delivering the actual test. Some pre-assessment administration processes include providing test information (e.g., the nature and the criteria of the test and tasks, as well as any pre-test preparation) to students beforehand (via website, flyer, brochure, and/or information sessions). This information helps students orient and prepare to take the test. Drawing on O'Sullivan (2012, p. 53), in the actual assessment administration, the following should be considered:

1. *physical conditions*, such as the seating of students, lighting, noise control, and room temperature;
2. *uniformity of administration and invigilation*, including consistent monitoring of ongoing administration, proctoring, penalties for test cheating or dishonesty, timing, and time management;
3. *test security*, such as test delivery modes, storage of assessments or tests before and after administration, and where to safeguard students' data.

To succeed in these aspects, it is essential to provide clear instructions for proctors and/or administrators, so that they understand what they have to do to deliver and moderate the assessment, including checking students' identities and informing them at the beginning about what will happen if they engage in dishonest conduct. Assessment administrators must report any administrative problems impacting students' performance to the responsible designer or teacher.

Another crucial administrative consideration is ensuring that *accommodations* are provided and administered adequately to students with disabilities (discussed further in Section 6.5 as part of assessment qualities). Students with disabilities or special needs may take the test separately owing to their specific requirements. In non-test assessments, accommodations can be arranged similarly for students where appropriate, and special considerations such as extension of time owing to students' illness, injury, or misadventure can be provided.

6.1.4 Stage 4 (Score)

There are three main types of scoring method: objective, semi-objective, and subjective.

- *Objective scoring* refers to scoring that does not require raters' judgements. That is, answer keys can be used for scoring. Restricted-response techniques (e.g., multiple-choice and true/false) are scored objectively.
- *Semi-objective scoring* suggests that there can be some variation in the correct answers or responses. Short constructed-response techniques such as *short-answer* questions and *cloze* or *gap-filling* tasks may involve *semi-objective scoring* as correct answers can appear in variable forms (e.g., word choices and grammatical correctness of responses) that require informed rater judgements. Some constructed-response tasks, such as *dictation*, may be considered semi-objective scoring as acceptable responses are pre-identified (see further discussion on the dictation technique in Section 5.1.6 under 'Constructed-Response Techniques').
- *Subjective scoring* requires scorers or raters to make their judgements on responses. Usually, performance assessments such as direct speaking and writing tasks require *subjective scoring*. The term subjective is used because test scores are based on scorers' or raters' perceptions about the quality of the performance. It is subjective because there can be variations in test scores. For example, two raters may assign the same performance different scores. In subjective scoring, scoring rubrics and rater moderation can help ensure consistency (Galaczi & Lim, 2022; Pill & Smart, 2021).

6.1.5 Stage 5 (Use)

Finally, assessment use should correspond to the intended purpose(s) identified earlier in the planning stage. We note that the reasoning underpinning this stage is applicable to both tests and non-test assessments. Once students' responses are scored, teachers decide their success (e.g., pass/fail, admit/not admit, employ/not employ, and so on). In language education, decisions based on assessment can go beyond simply a pass-fail decision (e.g., awarding different grades). If there is a limited number of positions available, scores are typically ranked, and candidates with the highest test scores are generally considered for selection (as discussed in the NRA).

In summary, developing summative tests or assessments is a complex process. Typically, the development of standardised testing for large-scale assessment is not a task for a teacher working on their own; it requires teamwork and expert knowledge, with each team member responsible for leading a specific stage. To learn more about the stages discussed in this section, see Bachman and Damböck (2017), Davidson and Lynch (2002), and Green (2020).

Test Development
https://bit.ly/47wD2X9

6.1.6 Types of Test Techniques

This section presents examples of selected- and constructed-response techniques teachers may consider in their question (also known as 'test item') design (see Brown & Abeywickrama, 2019; Purpura, 2016; Weir, 1990, 2005 for a comprehensive discussion of test and assessment techniques).

Selected-Response Techniques

In selected-response techniques, students are limited in how they can respond to questions or tasks. Such techniques include discrete-point techniques such as checklists, analogies, multiple-choice, true/false, and matching. These techniques are often used for assessing receptive language skills or linguistic knowledge (e.g., grammar and vocabulary) because the focus is often on comprehension, understanding, and/or identification. The following are selected examples of this technique.

a. A *dichotomous technique* (e.g., yes/no, true/false, A/B, present/absent) can be used to assess receptive skills but is unsuitable for assessing productive skills. A test using this technique is relatively easy to construct (e.g., ideas or information from the text can be presented as statements with prompts) and quick to score. In FA, teachers can use this technique to check students' understanding in the classroom. In binary or dichotomous items, e.g., yes/no questions, students have a 50 per cent chance of being correct using blind guessing – a source of error in scores. They may answer incorrectly owing to flaws, a lack of clarity, or inaccuracy in the statement, and they may obtain the correct answer for the wrong reason or by merely picking randomly. Teachers can use FA techniques to overcome this by asking students to explain their answers. Providing grounds for answers is an extra task that requires reflexive thinking skills and additional writing requirements.

b. A *multiple-choice technique* is often adopted in language assessment. These items allow students to select an answer from three to five choices, although four may be the most common. The popularity of this technique is driven by the practical nature of its administration and scoring, especially in large-scale standardised assessments. This technique can test a broad range of reading and listening constructs or knowledge of productive skills such as grammatical, vocabulary, pronunciation, and pragmatic ability. Figure 8 illustrates an example of a multiple-choice reading comprehension test.

   As with the dichotomous techniques, students are asked to choose only one of the multiple options as the correct answer. It is essential to pre-test, edit, and check the difficulty levels and distractor functions for this type of test. The sole use of and reliance on this technique in a test has been criticised and discouraged (Alderson, 2000). For instance, there is the possibility of guessing. Even when five-choice questions are used, the chance of being correct by guessing is 20 per cent, so the effect of guessing is not negligible. Furthermore, the choosing activities are unnatural in real-world language use (e.g., people are rarely given options in real-life conversations). It is, therefore, difficult to generalise high test scores to real-life language use success.

c. A *checklist technique* is used to ask students to select and produce a list of items of information based on a reading or listening text (e.g., check all that are relevant to the question). Checklists can assess scanning and skimming skills and the accuracy of information retrieval and retention. Figure 9 provides an example of a checklist technique.

   Partial correctness can be used in scoring this technique, though this may result in a complex procedure. In FA, checklists are useful for checking students' knowledge and understanding. For example, in FA of writing, a list can be used to remind students whether they have completed or engaged in some activities (e.g., ☑ I have checked subject–verb agreements; ☑ I have

Instructions: Read the following passage. Answer the questions based on what is stated or implied in the text. Choose the best answer A, B, C or D to each question.

Most of us at some point in our lives, most frequently during our school years, find ourselves struggling to learn foreign vocabulary. As you have probably discovered for yourself, learning new words is generally a very time-consuming and effortful business. Interestingly, in their research in 1975, Atkinson and Raugh found that the keyword technique was a useful way of making it easier to acquire or learn foreign vocabulary. In this technique, for example, native English learners first of all form an association between each spoken foreign word and an English word or phrase sounding like it and its English equivalent. For example, the Russian word *zvonok* is pronounced *zvah-oak* and means bell. This can be learned by using an oak tree covered with bells.

***Source**: Extract adapted from Baddeley et al. (2009, p. 374).*

1. What is the main topic of this passage?
   A. How to pronounce the Russian word zvonok.
   B. Problems in learning new foreign vocabulary.
   C. A technique for learning foreign vocabulary.
   D. Who discovered the keyword technique?

Answer: C

Figure 8 Example of a multiple-choice test

According to information given in the conversation between Thomas and Jane, put a tick (✓) next to what Thomas has planned to do on Saturday. There may more than one answer.

□ Go to the beach
□ Go to the dentist
□ Do some gardening
□ Get a haircut
□ Go shopping

Figure 9 Example of a test using a checklist technique

checked my spelling before submitting). Test instructions need to be precise because students may understand the written or spoken text but may be confused by the instructions provided. For example, some students may believe that they must choose just one item in the given list (as in multiple-choice tests) when they need to select more than one, and this leads to failure.

Constructed-Response Techniques

Constructed-response techniques ask students to produce answers or responses on their own. Compared to the selected-response techniques, these minimise the effect of guessing. These techniques can be used to elicit short or extended responses. *Short constructed-response techniques* are, for instance, short-answer questions (e.g., one word only, or no more than three words), cloze or gap-filling (e.g., one word per one missing space in a text), and diagram completion (e.g., no more than three words). These techniques are somewhat restricting and controlling. The following are examples of this technique in more detail:

a. A *cloze technique* is mainly used for assessing reading skills. Every *nth* word (e.g., every fifth, sixth, or seventh word) in a paragraph is deleted, and students must devise a word to replace it. This technique taps into students' broad comprehension of the stimulus text. They have to work out what might be missing that could complete the meaning. When they complete the gap, they must pay attention to content meaning, grammatical features (e.g., tenses, verb forms), and word forms (e.g., plurals, nouns, adjectives, or adverbs). Figure 10 presents an example of a cloze technique in which every sixth word is removed.

   This technique can infer students' ability to understand text coherence since a word that correctly fills a given space needs to be meaningful and

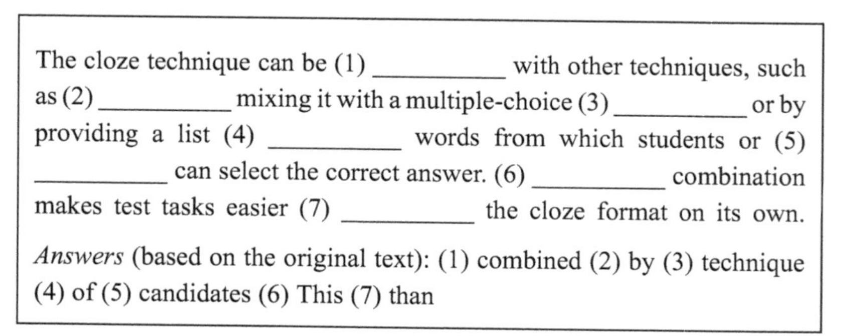

The cloze technique can be (1) __________ with other techniques, such as (2) __________ mixing it with a multiple-choice (3) __________ or by providing a list (4) __________ words from which students or (5) __________ can select the correct answer. (6) __________ combination makes test tasks easier (7) __________ the cloze format on its own.

Answers (based on the original text): (1) combined (2) by (3) technique (4) of (5) candidates (6) This (7) than

Figure 10 Example of a test using a cloze technique

fit logically with the remaining parts of the sentence or paragraph. This technique, hence, requires the integrative skills discussed in Section 4.2.2. The cloze technique can be combined with other techniques, such as multiple-choice or providing a list of words to select the correct answer from. This technique can give students corrective feedback in FA because they must notice their vocabulary, grammar, spelling, and reading comprehension. The cloze technique, however, is known to lack authenticity in the sense that in ordinary real-life reading, not every *nth* word is missing; therefore, assessing reading this way requires more than reading ability since this is also a problem-solving activity.

b. A *gap-filling technique* can have different variants ranging from one word only to a few words. A one-word gap-filling technique is similar to a cloze technique, but a particular word is selected to be removed. That is, word deletion is motivated by assessment objectives, whereas the cloze technique is more format-driven (i.e., deleting every *n*th word) as the cloze technique. A gap-filling technique can assess reading and other language-using skills, such as listening, writing, and speaking, as well as grammatical knowledge. In listening, students can fill in a gap in a written text, diagram, or graph as they listen to the audio passage. This technique can be successfully employed in dictations in which students listen to an audio text and fill in the missing words according to what is heard. This is also known as *partial dictation*. In writing, they may complete a form or application. In speaking, they may complete a conversation (e.g., what the person will likely say after a question in a discourse completion task). Discourse completion tasks are indirect assessments of speaking. In a grammar test, they may complete a space that makes the sentence grammatically correct.

c. A *short-answer technique* is considered to be a semi-objective, constructed-response technique. Assessments using this technique involve students giving responses that are somewhat restricted. This technique can assess reading or listening comprehension skills (e.g., what, where, when, why, and how questions). The number of words for short answers can vary but should range between three and six in reading or listening tests. Long answers will shift students' attention from listening to writing answers in listening assessment. The writing-up of 'long' answers is likely to be *construct-irrelevant* (i.e., the ability has nothing to do with listening comprehension skills). In some reading tests, students can write a sentence or two as their answers. Again, the instructions for students regarding the length of response required should be explicit and easy to understand to avoid misunderstanding, leading to failures.

An *information-transfer technique* is a variant of the short constructed-response technique. This technique is usually linked to visual representations or mind maps of texts. In a reading or listening test, students read or listen to a text and complete a graph, diagram, chart, or table with missing information, for example.

A short-answer technique can also be applied in speaking assessment. Students may complete a series of questions by responding to them verbally (e.g., What's your name? Where do you come from? What is your favourite subject this semester?). Such a test inevitably involves listening skills since students need to be able to understand questions before they can answer them. In a pronunciation test, tasks that require reading aloud a series of words, phrases, or sentences may be considered a short-answer technique. In a writing test, a short-answer technique is exemplified by completing a form or application. It can also ask students to construct a sentence based on the provided words.

The target skill or ability assessed through constructed-response techniques depends on other language and/or cognitive skills not directly assessed. For example, in a listening test, skills other than listening skills include reading comprehension and writing, as students need to read questions and options or write answers to questions.

Extended constructed-response techniques require students to produce lengthier answers or responses (e.g., essays, interviews, role plays, oral presentations). These techniques can assess productive skills such as writing and speaking.

a. A *pictures or events description technique* is an extended constructed-response technique. However, responses remain somewhat restricted because students can only speak or write what a series of sequentially ordered pictures or events suggests. At the same time, students need to construct their own spoken or written discourse as they describe the pictures or events. To achieve this task, students need to have sufficient vocabulary knowledge related to the photographs or events and the grammatical ability to construct their speech or sentences. This technique is suitable for specific-purpose tests. For example, a doctor may need to explain a series of medical procedures to colleagues or patients; a chef may explain the steps in which a particular dish is to be prepared; and a tourist guide can explain the history of a tourist destination or cultural artefact. Since all students describe the same pictures or events, scoring is less complicated than scoring for

Instructions: Look at the picture below. You are to talk about what you can see. You have 30 seconds to look at the picture carefully and to prepare what to include in your talk. You will have 30 seconds to complete your talk. You should speak clearly and not rush. Start with the words '*In the picture, I can see ....*'

Figure 11 A speaking task based on a picture

interview or role-play techniques. Figure 11 provides an example of a picture task for a speaking test.

There are some cautions to keep in mind when using a picture or events task. For instance, students' performance may depend on the quality of the pictures used and their content-specific knowledge. They may not interpret the pictures or events in the same way as the test designers, teachers, or essay markers. Furthermore, pictures may be culturally sensitive regardless of test designers' best attempts to find culturally neutral scenes. A picture that puts test-takers in a negative frame of mind is unlikely to elicit their optimal performance. Finally, some students may be more creative than others when describing pictures or telling events. However, creativity may not be a construct of interest in the assessment.

b. A *dictation technique* is an integrative constructed-response technique that requires students to listen to a read-aloud text and then write what they have heard verbatim. Students use listening, reading, and writing skills as well as memorisation (which may not be a relevant construct of interest that differentiates performance). Once the appropriateness of the content of the dictation passage has been checked, the difficulty levels are determined simply by deciding whether the text is read once or twice and whether the reading speed is slow, moderate, or fast. Partial dictation, which may involve students writing a phrase or sentences in specific areas in a given text, may be considered to reduce writing volume. Figure 12 is an example of a partial dictation technique.

Instructions: You are to listen to a talk about the use of dictation tests to control immigration in Australia. You are to write down **exactly** what you have heard in the missing spaces. First, the text will be read once at a natural speed; second, the text will be read with a pause between sentences; third, the text will be read again at a natural speed. You should check your spelling and use of capital letters.

Test-takers hear:

The 'White Australia Policy' and the dictation test under which it was infamously enforced provided central policy tools in the quest to control Australia's immigrant population from Federation in 1901 until well into the twentieth century. The dictation test, which was a key element of the Immigration Restriction Act 1901, has always been associated with the question of race.

It was administered to 'coloureds' and 'Asians' in order to have an apparently neutral reason to deport them. The last person to pass the test did so in 1909. It became foolproof, as it was designed to be. The applicant would be given the test in a language that their background firmly indicated they would not know and, upon failing, they would be told that the authorities could go on giving them tests in languages that they did not know, infinitely.

Test-takers see:

The 'White Australia Policy' and the dictation test under which it was infamously enforced provided central policy tools in the quest to (1) ____

______________________________________ until well into the twentieth century. The dictation test, which was a key element of the Immigration Restriction Act 1901, (2) ______________

____

____.

Figure 12 (cont.) 15

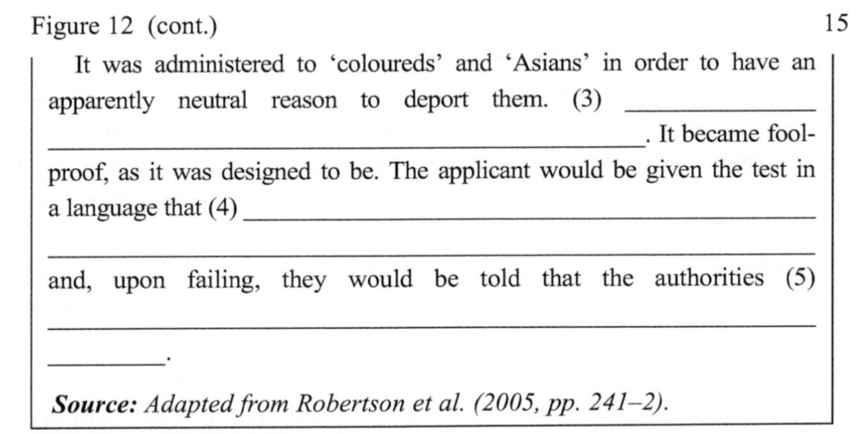
It was administered to 'coloureds' and 'Asians' in order to have an apparently neutral reason to deport them. (3) ______________________________. It became foolproof, as it was designed to be. The applicant would be given the test in a language that (4) ______________________________ and, upon failing, they would be told that the authorities (5) ______________________________.

Source: *Adapted from Robertson et al. (2005, pp. 241–2).*

Figure 12 Example of a partial dictation test

The feedback on performance involving dictation or partial dictation can be formative. A dictation test can help students improve their working memory, self-monitoring and self-assessment, and fluent recall of information. In scoring, issues such as spelling mistakes and other writing skills (e.g., capitalisation and tenses) should be considered and addressed.

c. A *summary technique* can assess receptive and productive language skills. It assesses integrative skills. The focus, however, is on accuracy in expressing, summarising, or paraphrasing the main ideas, sequences, and essential information from a text. A summary technique can be combined with the dictation technique. Students read and summarise a text through writing or speaking. Instructions must ensure that students understand the requirement (e.g., Write no more than 50 words; Speak within 30 seconds after the beep sound.).
d. A *free-verbal* or *free-written recall technique* is a variant of the dictation and summary technique. This is an extended integrative technique for assessing reading, listening, speaking, or writing. In a reading or listening test, students read or listen to a text and then speak or write about what they have understood from their reading or listening. This type of assessment focusses on accurate comprehension of a given text. In a speaking assessment, in addition to correct recollections of information, the assessment can focus on the intelligibility of speech, pronunciation, and fluency. In writing tests, the assessment criteria can include content accuracy, spelling, grammatical accuracy, vocabulary use, and mechanics (e.g., punctuation). This technique can become an *integrated task* when students are required to add or relate their position to the topic and their examples or support in an essay or speech. This technique seems natural

in the sense that there are no test questions that intervene in students' receptive or productive language processes.

In SA, performance is, however, dependent on task familiarity, practice, memory capacity, and the topics and the complexity of texts. Some students can comprehend a text well while reading or listening but may struggle to remember what they have just read or heard shortly after finishing reading or listening. In a reading or listening assessment, this technique may not reveal students' natural ways of reading or listening because they do not usually need to tell people what and how much they can recall. The relevance of this technique for FA is that it helps students learn to use memory strategies, which are essential for enhancing language learning and use. Teachers can help students with feedback and memory strategy instructions. Students can practise recalling what they have read or heard, and they can start with simple texts, then move to more complex and lengthier texts.

e. An *essay technique* is a flexible constructed-response method for assessing writing. Generally, students are asked to independently write an essay responding to a statement or question (see integrated tasks in Section 4.2.2). Essay topics can range from personal topics, such as my last holiday, my hobby, or my family, to academic or social topics, such as issues in climate change, technology, education, or social issues. In EMI and CLIL settings, essays are most likely to be subject topic–related. Students are expected to state their position, provide support, reasons, and examples, and organise an essay based on what they have been taught (e.g., introduction–body–conclusion). As far as possible, it would be advisable to avoid offensive topics that may impact negatively on student performance. Instructions need to be explicit and transparent (e.g., the number of words students need to write, the time allowance, and the criteria used to judge their essays).

f. A *role-play technique* is used frequently for assessing speaking as it is adaptable for various student or test-taker levels. This technique is commonly used in standardised language proficiency tests and can be suitable for scenario-based assessment. It is versatile and communication-oriented to capture various speaking repertoires, from basic pronunciations to pragmatic and turn-taking skills. It is often used in specific-purpose assessments (e.g., business English, English for aviation and medical professionals). Students imagine themselves being in a specific role in a given scenario and use the target language to exchange information or solve a problem, for instance. A role-play technique can be carried out between an interviewer (examiner) and a student or test-taker, or it can be assigned in a pair-speaking task in which two students are responsible for a particular role.

Similar to the essay technique, instructions must be clear regarding the criteria for evaluating performance and the preparation time and time for task completion.

g. *Oral presentation*: Oral presentation is a versatile and authentic technique for assessing speaking and communication skills and content knowledge. In professional and educational contexts (e.g., meetings, conferences, advertisements, product or service promotions), oral presentations are common. In classroom contexts, oral presentations can be part of a larger project or assessed coursework students have been working on. Students can present a topic with or without a PowerPoint presentation or other audiovisual or multimedia aids. Students need to understand task requirements and practise before their oral presentations.

   In some educational contexts, for example in some Italian universities, final degree exams can involve oral presentations to the professor, which is, in effect, a verbal essay on a topic. For example, there is an element of oral presentations in North American, New Zealand, and UK university practice for PhD viva voce. Such oral presentations typically include a question-and-answer session after the presentation. Oral presentations can also be included as part of paired or group work, as they can involve collaboration and leadership. That said, they can also be challenging for some students owing to a lack of language proficiency and collegiality with group members.

6.2 Non-test Assessment Design

Standardised summative tests follow specific stages in design, development, and administration. Therefore, while some considerations in test design can be applicable for non-test assessments (e.g., planning, designing, and evaluating), other considerations differ significantly because, typically, non-test assessment tasks can serve both formative and summative purposes. Unlike standardised tests focussing on individual students, non-test assessments can be conducted as pair or group tasks.

6.2.1 Contemporary Approaches to FA

This section explores four approaches that can inform FA practices: dynamic assessment, learning-oriented assessment, usage-based, and scenario-based assessments. In the language assessment literature, these assessment approaches have been discussed in relation to assessment for and of learning.

Dynamic Assessment

Dynamic assessment focusses on the development and processes of learning during teacher-guided activities. Generally speaking, it tends to focus on an individual student who is regarded unique in their language learning needs and their ability to tackle a learning task successfully. When students encounter difficulties, teachers provide scaffolding and feedback to support task engagement, considering the student's current knowledge and ability. Guidance is fine-tuned to each student's particular learning needs or difficulties with the learning task. The aim is not to spoon-feed students in terms of how to correct their errors but to provide advice on how to address problems, taking account of their learning dispositions. Teacher feedback in dynamic assessment should be premised on a clear view of the learning processes or steps involved. To achieve this, teachers have to analyse and understand the nature of learning involved in any pedagogic task. This feature makes dynamic assessment different from other kinds of formative support. The principles of dynamic assessment have been extended to cover whole class teaching contexts. See Poehner and Infante (2017) for further discussion.

Dynamic assessment for speech
https://bit.ly/47oUBIw

Learning-Oriented Assessment

Learning-oriented assessment (LoA) takes a learning approach in which the real-life educational environment (e.g., learning outcomes, mandatory internal and external assessments), cognition (e.g., thinking processes required to develop and learn the target language features), affect of students (e.g., feeling and emotion), and social contexts (classroom settings, teachers and peers) are considered (Carless, 2007, 2015; Turner & Purpura, 2017). Thus, LoA can involve a cycle of teaching, learning, and assessment both inside and outside the classroom, and it can use all forms of assessment, including both FA and SA. For example, it can begin with teachers using the learning outcomes or objectives to develop teaching, learning, and assessment activities (e.g., how to engage in small talk). Students are then introduced to the concept of small talk with real-life examples of small talk. They work individually, in pairs, or in groups to learn from the examples. After that, they are encouraged to personalise their own small talk. In-class activities include teachers monitoring student learning, tracking student progress, and providing feedback on their learning and performance (e.g., suggesting correct pronunciation or word choice). Self- and peer-assessment can also be promoted as students complete learning activities. Teachers can also use SA techniques, such as quizzes and achievement tests, and non-test assessment tasks, such as project-based and portfolio assessments, to help students realise real-life applications of small talk. Both FA and SA techniques can be aligned with the learning outcomes or objectives. In out-of-class activities, students are invited to engage in independent study projects (on topics and materials guided by teachers). They may be encouraged to use digital technology to conduct their studies multimodally. Teachers can also offer a follow-up discussion with students about their out-of-class learning during class time. The fundamental premise of LoA is that students should learn new skills or useful knowledge while participating in assessment activities. In LoA, targeted language-use scenarios are adopted to ensure that the learning activities meet students' personal, educational, and social goals as appropriate. See Chong and Reinders (2023), Jones and Saville (2016), and Turner and Purpura (2017) for further discussion.

SCAN ME 15

The different stages of the LoA cycle
https://bit.ly/3SdbnG8

Usage-Based Assessment

Ellis et al. (2015) and Douglas Fir Group (2016) discuss a theoretical framework that describes and explains the nature of language use as language learning. This framework postulates that people recognise the function of language through how it is used. For example, frequently or repeatedly used language features in a given context are likely to be more noticed in terms of how and what they are used for than those infrequently used. This idea recognises that language use in a real-life activity is often patterned (see Cadierno & Eskildsen, 2015; Dolgova & Tyler, 2019; Hall, 2019). For that reason, concepts in usage-based language learning have implications for language teaching and assessment in terms of what to teach and assess. For example, Thai students learning to use English in Thailand require different foci on content and activities from those studying English in England because the needs for and exposures to English usage are different. Therefore, usage-based assessment should be sensitive to local language use and learning.

Scenario-Based Assessment

Purpura (2021) provides a useful discussion of scenario-based assessment. A scenario is an imaginary language-use scene that is used to generate a real-life experience in which a student interacts with a task. The task may include a collaborative activity among students and teachers. Language use in a given scenario can be dynamic and flexible. Purpura (2021) operationalises scenario-based assessment through computer technology, although it can be carried out in an in-person classroom. Scenario-based assessment focusses on using real-life, interconnected tasks. For example, in academic language use, students are likely to engage in various tasks both individually and in groups. They later create a nexus of interconnected language use to accomplish a larger communicative goal. Students may read several texts about a topic of interest and watch a documentary or news about that topic, and so forth, to discuss main issues with other students and professors. Before that, they may summarise key messages from various resources through notes or texts. They may read their summaries aloud to rehearse their speech or check their intelligibility. This example shows that different language uses are integrated or combined to serve a meaningful overall purpose.

These four assessment approaches are relevant to effective classroom language teaching and assessment. They share three common concerns. First, it is vital to help students imagine a real-life language-use situation they will face and to relate their language learning and use to such a situation. Second, various multimodal learning and assessment tasks can be created as a pedagogic space (comprising tasks of increasing complexity) in which students can connect smaller pieces or segments to form a larger language-use goal for a specific purpose or scenario. Third, students can receive feedback on language use as part of their engagement with the assessment activities.

6.2.2 General Considerations for Non-test SA Tasks

The following are some significant non-test SA design features that are relevant to the four approaches discussed above. We focus on assessments that will contribute to student attainment or achievement decision-making.

1. Assessment tasks should be conceptualised as an integral part of a syllabus design, paying particular attention to their purposes, suitability, and meaningfulness for students and their alignments with the learning outcomes. Teachers need to calculate the relative contributions of various assessment tasks to students' final grades.
2. Instructions for each assessment task should be explicit and clear. Students need to know the purpose of a given task and what they need to do to meet the task requirements (e.g., structures or components of their work, word counts (for written work), other materials to be included, and assessment criteria). Students should be clear on whether, for example, generative artificial intelligence (AI) is allowed to help them complete their assigned task. They also need to know the timeline for completion and checklists, including the due date and how to seek help when they have questions. If students are asked to submit various stages of their drafts for feedback, specific dates should be provided. Figure 13 presents an example of a timeline for students to follow when working on a piece of coursework.
3. Asessment rubrics should be carefully developed to assess various aspects of students' submitted work. Rubrics should provide transparency in terms of expectations. Teachers should explain the rubrics and promote how students can use them to self-assess their ongoing and final work (see Brown, 2012 for rubric development and use in LTA). Figure 14 provides an example of an assessment rubric that evaluates various aspects of students' submitted work.
4. Students should receive a final grade/score on their submitted work as well as formative and summative feedback, such as strengths and points for improvement (see Section 7 on feedback).

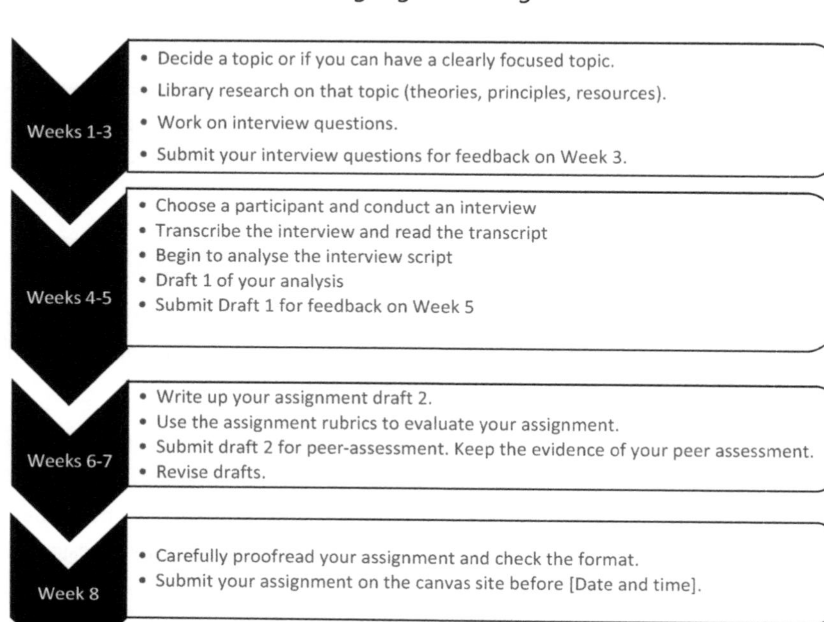

Figure 13 Timeline for completing a piece of coursework

6.2.3 Examples of Non-test Assessment Tasks

The following provides an overview of non-test assessment tasks that have gained popularity in classroom assessments because they promote task authenticity, integrated language skills, application skills, and creativity. Students are not constrained by the extent of time pressure as they are in a standardised test condition.

Portfolio Assessment

Portfolio assessment is a broad approach that focusses on a collection of students' work over time (e.g., an assigned task that cannot be completed in standardised conditions). It can accommodate collections of separate or integrated language skills. It takes a learner-centred approach to assessment because it focusses on students' ongoing learning processes and the outcomes of such processes. Therefore, students collect various drafts and outlines of their work that have been commented on for improvement, the materials they have used and produced, and their reflections as they completed the assessment task. Portfolios can be constructed in the form of physical folders or artefacts. E-portfolios are portfolios that embrace computer and information technology as well as cloud-based storage and sharing. E-portfolios have gained popularity

Subject & Task Fulfilment (30%) **Point:** _______	**Excellent** *30 to >25.5* Exceptionally fulfils the task requirements.	**Very Good** *25.5 to >22.5* Largely fulfils the task requirements very well.	**Good** *22.5 to >19.5* Competently fulfils the task requirements.	**Fair** *19.5 to >15* Fulfils the minimum task requirements.	**Fail** *15 to >0* Does not fulfil the task requirements.
Appraisals (25%) **Point:** _______	*25 to >21.25* Effectively and suitably uses and evaluates sources and information to support the purpose of the task.	*21.25 to >18.75* Uses and evaluates sources and information very well to support the purpose of the task.	*18.75 to >16.25* Competently uses and evaluates sources and information to address the purpose of the task.	*16.25 to >12.5* Meets the minimum expectation of sources and information use and evaluation.	*12.5 to 0* Does not use or evaluate sources and information to serve the purpose of the task.
Analysis (25%) **Point:** _______	*25 to >21.25* Effectively analyses the interview to support the research question.	*21.25 to >18.75* Analyses the interview to support the research question very well.	*18.75 to >16.25* Competently analyses the interview to support the research question.	*16.25 to >12.5* Meets the minimum requirements for interview analysis.	*12.5 to 0* Does not meet the minimum requirements for interview analysis.
Organisation (10%) **Point:** _______	*10 to >8.5* Effectively follows the assignment structural guideline. Shows superior organisational and conceptual skills.	*8.5 to >7.5* Largely follows the assignment structural guideline. Shows very good organisational and conceptual skills.	*7.5 to >6.5* Competently follows the assignment structural guideline, although some sections are not as effective.	*6.5 to >5* Meets the minimum assignment structural guideline.	*5 to >0* Does not follow, or deviates significantly from, the assignment structural guideline. Several aspects may be largely confused or undeveloped.
Writing Quality (10%) **Point:** _______	*10 to >8.5* Shows superior clarity in expressions, with attention to detail in all aspects evident.	*8.5 to >7.5* Uses a fluent and succinct style appropriate to the assessment task. Grammar, spelling, use of language, and punctuation are mostly appropriate and accurate.	*7.5 to >6.5* Shows mainly clear, fluent, and appropriate expression. Grammar, spelling, use of language, and punctuation are generally accurate.	*6.5 to >5* Uses some unclear expressions. Some flaws exist in grammar, spelling, use of language, and punctuation.	*5 to >0* Some apparent meaning emerges but is largely not fluently or clearly expressed. Grammar, spelling, language, and/or punctuation are poor.

Figure 14 Assessment rubric (based on an assessment rubric of an English for academic purposes unit of study)

as they are flexible regarding simultaneous and synchronous student–student or student–teacher communication (see Lam, 2023 for further discussion).

Task-Based Assessment

Task-based assessment is directly related to a task-based language teaching approach, which focusses on helping students learn and use the target language communicatively in authentic language-use situations. Task-based teaching and learning is a communicative approach to language teaching and learning that focusses on fulfilling communicative tasks. It does not ignore the importance of raising awareness of relevant linguistic form that makes language use accurate and/ or appropriate (i.e., focus on form). Task accomplishment tends to be integrative and integrated as students must combine various language skills for successful communication. Task-based language assessment can be both formative and summative as students can receive feedback on their performance to improve their communicative skills, contributing to overall learning attainment. Task-based assessment may be designed similarly to portfolio assessment, but students may not be required to submit all their drafts and other artefacts for evaluation. Instead, the focus may be on the outcome of fulfilling the task rather than on the detailed processes and development that led to the outcome, as in portfolio assessment.

Reflection Box 5

Is it necessary to plan an SA for a language classroom? Why or why not? Share your thoughts here: https://bit.ly/46WJmXw.

7 Quality Aspects in Assessment

Several frameworks for considering the quality and the practice of testing and assessment are available in the language assessment literature (e.g., Bachman & Palmer, 2010; Green, 2020; ILTA, 2020; Kunnan, 2018). This section presents six quality criteria (see Figure 15).

7.1 Reliability (Revisited)

We have introduced the concept of reliability under CTT in regard to measurement errors. Reliability relates to how assessment practices and results are consistent in standardised tests. In SA, we can think of reliability as the level of consistency of

Figure 15 Six interrelated quality criteria for testing and assessment practice

students' performance. When students complete the same test, they should perform similarly today, yesterday, and tomorrow. If students pass the test today but fail the same test tomorrow, then there is a problem with reliability. We cannot rely on this test for decision-making. In statistics, a reliability estimate of a test ranges from 0 (completely unreliable or random) to 1 (completely reliable). A reliability estimate of 0.90 is expected for tests used to make a high-stakes decision.

It is important to note that the concepts of reliability in CTT cannot be applied to some aspects of classroom assessment, such as learning-oriented, formative, and dynamic assessment. It is unreasonable to expect that students' performances can be consistently measured because they are developing their knowledge and skills. Their performances can fluctuate over time and across contexts and tasks. Similarly, in portfolio assessment, much of students' work can be in the form of drafts and revised drafts, so their performances cannot be expected to be consistent. Therefore, in learning-oriented or dynamic assessment, *trustworthiness* is more appropriately used. The notion of 'trustworthiness' in language assessment refers to the quality of assessment activities that can be dependable, useful, and relevant to teaching and learning activities.

7.2 Validity

In the mainstream language assessment literature, validity refers to the extent to which scores infer the target ability or construct and are used appropriately and ethically in decision-making (Chapelle, 2021; Chapelle & Lee, 2022; Phakiti & Isaacs, 2021). In this section, we explain three aspects of validity that are relevant for consideration in FA and SA: construct, content, and face validity.

1. Construct validity: Constructs are theoretical and abstract concepts that cannot be observed directly. When we use scores to indicate students' abilities or skills, we can ask *whether the test or assessment accurately and appropriately captures the abstract abilities or skills that we claim to be testing or assessing*. If so, what evidence do we have to support our claim? The same question can be applied to classroom assessment. The focus of assessment should always be aligned with assessment tasks, be they in the form of test questions or portfolios compiled by students.
2. Content validity: We all know that examinations and tests are unusually concerned with a particular subject or area of knowledge and skills. So, the selection and the design of test/exam items (questions) have to tap into the focal construct. Content validity refers to the extent to which the tasks and activities involved in assessment are linked to the focal construct. Therefore, only sample tasks or activities relevant to and representative of the target

constructs should be used. Therefore, content validity can be thought of as *the extent to which the content of the test is relevant and sufficient to assess the target constructs of interest*. By relevance, we mean that assessment tasks or questions must prompt students to produce the language related to the target constructs or abilities. For example, suppose teachers give students a multiple-choice grammar test and use the scores to infer the extent of their speaking skills. In that case, the test is both construct and content invalid simply because knowledge of grammar does not equate to speaking skills, and the tasks cannot elicit samples of the speaking skills. By sufficiency, we mean obtaining an adequate amount and quality of task responses from students to enable evaluation and making an evidence-based decision. This consideration applies to both standardised testing and classroom assessment. In classroom assessment, content validity can be checked by asking whether test tasks or questions are similar to what students have done in the classroom. If they are not, then there are issues with the content validity.

3. Face validity: Generally, this refers to the appearance or perceived relevance of the assessment or test to stakeholders including teachers, students, university administrators, employers, and possibly even the general public. If a test or assessment task does not look as though it measures what it claims to measure, it does not have face validity. We used an example of a grammar test to claim about students' speaking ability in Point (2), which lacks both construct and content validity. This is also an example of a test that lacks face validity. In addition, face validity can be considered in terms of assessment formats, sequences of tasks, and how fairness and test security are addressed. Although the primary focus of language assessment should be construct and content validity, it is undeniable that *face validity* is essential.

SCAN ME 16

What every teacher needs to know about assessment
https://bit.ly/3Nkw8gk

7.3 Practicality

In language assessment, ideally, we would like to collect as much language and language-related information as possible to have confidence in our decisions. Nonetheless, there is a need to consider whether such an expectation is realistic because assessment needs to be practical. The term *practicality* is related to the extent to which an assessment is feasible in a given context. In both FA and SA, teachers need to consider the *cost*, *resources*, and *time* required and constrained to develop, administer, and score or evaluate students' responses.

The practicality considerations of FA differ from those of SA in various ways. For example, classroom AfL is ongoing and embedded in teaching and learning activities. The teaching and learning activities, whether in-person or online, are designed to lead to qualitative feedback to the students. Thus, AfL can be time-demanding for teachers and students. It may not be practical to give individualised feedback to each student. In SA, since the main assessment concern is mainly obtaining outcomes accurately and efficiently, test designers routinely consider how much time will be needed to develop a test or assessment task, how much time students will need to complete the test or assessment, and how much money will be spent on development and administration. Practicality considerations can also cover issues such as throughput efficiency (the number of students/test-takers per administration) and marking efficiency (use of machine marking or human raters). A lengthy and complex assessment can collect extensive evidence of learning, but it is more expensive and time-consuming to develop and administer. A shorter assessment may be time-efficient and affordable, but may not sufficiently collect students' knowledge or skills of interest.

7.4 Ethics

The issues of ethics and fairness impact the quality aspects of testing and assessment. These concepts are intertwined (see the International Language Testing Association (ILTA) Guidelines for Practice, which comprehensively cover ethical assessment). Generally speaking, the term 'ethics' concerns the broad educational principles and social responsibilities that assessment developers, curriculum designers, teachers, and policymakers have to address. Ethics are at the heart of testing and assessment practice. Ethical considerations are part of the decision-making when teachers or test developers select test questions or assessment tasks for a given purpose and group of students, decide on the marking and reporting framework, and design protocols for safeguarding students' personal and assessment data.

Teachers are expected to ensure that students learn as effectively as possible. It is considered unethical if teachers never monitor their students' learning. Using a range of assessment methods (e.g., questions, exercises, quizzes, homework) to help students engage in language learning activities allows teachers and students to find out what has been learnt and what has been a challenge. These are ways to establish trust, shared purpose, and collaboration in the classroom. Teachers can guide students to take responsibility for their own learning. For example, students can be taught to engage in self- and peer-assessment. As they become more and more independent, they begin to develop learner autonomy. These are ethical principles that have been embedded in FA.

But SA is imbued with ethical considerations too. For instance, final degree examinations are a means of providing accountability – examination results can be used as an indicator of the quality of the education programs involved. Ethical practice in SA includes:

1. designing and using tests and assessments relevant to the unit of study or the subject being taught. Using tests or assessments not aligned with the learning outcomes or the teaching and learning activities is unethical;
2. informing students about essential tests and assessments they must complete in the course and the consequences of not succeeding. Students should be aware of their assessment responsibilities;
3. reminding students of assessment dates and allowing them to ask questions to help them prepare for assessment tasks;
4. ensuring that students have equal access to essential resources for learning and attainment. Assessment is unfair if some students can access resources while others cannot;
5. conducting the SA in accordance with the appropriate rubrics and protocols within the given assessment framework. Making ungrounded, unfair, and prejudicial judgements on test performance is unethical;
6. providing feedback on students' performance individually or in groups so that they can confirm their understanding and realise critical areas they need to correct or improve on. In tests, quizzes, or assessments that produce scores, this includes providing numeric feedback with explanations of the scores that also cover areas of strength and weakness and what students should consider improving;
7. treating all students fairly, regardless of their ability level, gender, race/ethnicity, disabilities, religion, and socio-economic status;
8. calling out when dishonesty, such as cheating and plagiarism, is found. If such issues are not raised and addressed in accordance with the

established code of conduct, students who engage in such behaviours may think that it is acceptable to do so. Not doing anything about this is unethical because such an experience can engender further misdeeds. Furthermore, cheating, if unchecked, can result in unfairness for other students and test-takers.

7.5 Fairness

In the discussion on ethics in Section 6.4, issues of fairness are implicated. Fairness is related to equality of treatment and opportunity for all students (see Kunnan, 2018). In FA, for example, if teachers give detailed feedback and support only to some students, but not to others, they are unfair in their assessment practice. If a high-stakes SA offers advantages only to some students, but not to others (e.g., owing to gender, race, religion, or socio-economic status), it is not a fair assessment. An assessment can be considered unfair if the test items and tasks involve knowledge and skills that are accessible only to some of the students and/or test-takers, for example topics that some students may know more about owing to their backgrounds in terms of language, ethnicity/race, gender, religion, and socio-economic status (for further discussion, see Mirhosseini & De Costa, 2019). The following scenario illustrates how fairness and ethics can be intertwined, presenting plausible dilemmas that teachers may face.

> The school principal has decided that a computer-based test designed by a reputable testing company will be used in the final examination for the course. The argument for this decision is that it will save time for marking as scoring is automated, making the school look 'up-to-the-minute with technology' to the public. The teachers know that many students do not yet have sufficient skills to use computers and are from a low socio-economic background. Their students barely use computers to complete classroom tasks. The teachers also learn that none of the teaching and learning activities they have been covering in class are related to the test tasks and activities. There is a severe lack of alignment between the classroom activities and the test tasks. They fear that many students will fail if this computer-based test is used. This does not seem fair for students as the test content and the delivery method are inappropriate. Nonetheless, the teachers know that the school principal does not like people to disagree with their ideas; expressing such an opposing concern could mean running a career risk. If you were the teachers, what would you do?

In this scenario, the principal has not advanced a 'fairness' argument for the use of computer auto-marking. The professional dilemma for the teachers is whether to challenge the principal's authority. To do that might cause friction between the teachers and the principal. At the same time, the teachers cannot simply ignore the concerns; that course of (in)action might lead to students failing the test simply because it does not align with what they have been taught.

In many contemporary public education systems, schools and colleges serve minoritised students from diverse language backgrounds (e.g., some Hispanic backgrounds, Spanish-speaking communities in the USA, or speakers of indigenous languages in Australia). Suppose the language of academic communication is standard English (however defined). In that case, many minoritised students may receive unequal treatment and opportunity, particularly those at an early stage of learning English. For these students, the educational provision is unfair.

On a positive note, fairness can be facilitated by special considerations and accommodations. Considerations of *accommodations* for students with disabilities (both physical and cognitive diabilities) or those in difficult circumstances (e.g., unexpected illness or family tragedy) are essential (see Abedi, 2014; Abedi et al., 2020). Accommodations in language assessment may require some changes or modifications to the test questions, assessment tasks, administration conditions, and procedures. For example, accommodations may include extending the amount of time for completion of the test, allowing the use of text-to-speech software to read a text in a reading test or to produce speech in response to a speaking task, or providing an amanuensis (a person writing down answers for the student or test-taker).

7.6 Impact

Earlier in this Element, we discussed the meanings of 'stakes' in testing and assessment. Mandatory standardised tests can have a high impact on teachers as well as students. Teachers' careers may be impacted when their students perform poorly. Therefore, introducing a test or assessment will always have some degree of influence on the participants in various ways, as discussed earlier.

Test and assessment impact can be felt broadly by individual students, other stakeholders (e.g., teachers, schools, parents, employers), and society. Generally, *intended consequences* are directly related to using tests and assessments for a given purpose (e.g., to provide feedback to improve learning, to decide students' achievement or mastery of the learning outcomes, to certify, to admit, and to employ). *Unintended consequences* refer to the negative impacts of assessment use beyond intended results, for example the high-stakes nature of a given test or assessment causing cheating behaviours on the part of weak or low-ability students. Another example of unintended consequences of a high-stakes test is the massive use of private tutoring for test preparation, popularly known as 'cramming'.

We now focus on a well-recognised impact – washback (e.g., Tsagari & Cheng, 2017; Wall, 2012). Washback refers to the influences of tests or assessments on language teaching, learning, and/or curriculum design. For example, if a national language test is to be given to all students in their final year at school, teachers and students will pay attention to ways of maximising success. There may be extra teaching and learning activities to prepare students to take this test at the expense of other learning activities. This is an example of negative washback. In the language assessment literature, washback can be positive or negative.

- Positive washback refers to the impact of assessment that helps students progress, retaining or transferring what they have learnt. The test or assessment can prepare students to use the knowledge and skills in their future careers and lives. For example, if a test asks students to write or speak in the target language, they are likely to prepare themselves to do so. Consequently, this knowledge is also available for non-test language use after the test.
- Negative washback refers to a situation in which student learning is overly restricted to the knowledge and skills covered by a test or assessment task. In other words, the nature of the learning is curtailed to fit the parameters of the test. For example, a language assessment that measures only students' grammatical knowledge using a multiple-choice technique can have negative washback impact because isolated grammatical knowledge is insufficient for reading, listening, speaking, and writing in real-life contexts. Knowing grammar rules and how to answer multiple-choice questions is not sufficient for real-life language use or applications.

Scan Me 17

Positive washback
https://bit.ly/4aNCZsL

The concept of washback is relevant to both FA and SA. Teachers' AfL can have positive washback impacts on students' linguistic, cognitive, and social engagement. For example, when students receive some corrective feedback on their learning, they can realise their current difficulty or weakness and pay attention to improve it. This is an example of positive washback. When students are guided to become autonomous and self-regulated in their learning through the use of assessment criteria (often in the form of rubrics and sample questions/tasks), self-practices or rehearsals, and self-tests and assessments, they are likely to develop a capacity for autonomous learning as they have realised the benefits of self-monitoring and exploratory enquiry. The impact of assessment is omnipresent in formal education. The impact of assessment in English language education is most keenly felt in SA. The washback of large-scale commercially marketed tests such as IELTS and TOEFL often impacts the content of teaching programmes.

Reflection Box 6

Choose one of the quality criteria to focus on in a classroom assessment. How would you apply its principles in your assessment practice?

Share your thoughts here: https://bit.ly/3TkzqnK.

8 Further Developments

In this Element, we have explored functions and practices of language assessment, paying particular attention to the interconnections between FA and SA. We have discussed FA as embedded teaching and learning activities within a localised classroom for supporting and promoting learning. Teacher-led FA can respond to areas of students' learning and understanding that would benefit from further guidance and support. By contrast, SA mainly concerns pre-specified criteria of language ability, knowledge, skills, or learning outcomes. We have also presented a theoretical and technical discussion on what and how to assess in different contexts. We have foregrounded the significance and the impact of language assessment on education and society generally. We have drawn on conceptual and practical insights from language assessment research where appropriate.

In the next section, we articulate practical pedagogical implications, drawing on the insights and the principles of testing and assessment that we have presented. We share our thoughts on using formative feedback to improve students' learning, as well as guidelines for enhancing various types and forms of classroom assessment.

Section 7.2 focusses on the potential contributions of research and development for testing and assessment activities in language teaching. In Section 7.3, we provide recommendations for further professional development. A Glossary of Language Assessment and an Appendix are provided after this section.

8.1 Pedagogical Practice

8.1.1 Teaching and Assessment Alignments

Testing and assessment activities, for example AfL and AoL, serve various educational and professional functions and purposes. The alignment among them is often implicit. Many language curriculum specifications serve as teaching and learning objectives and as assessment criteria at the same time. Table 4 is an example of teaching–learning objectives that can also be used as assessment criteria.

8.1.2 Formative Feedback

Readers will notice that the discussion in this section on pedagogic practice contains some repetition of points made in other sections. We intend to make explicit the connections between theory and practice. Feedback matters in additional/second language acquisition (Gass et al., 2020). For example, it can raise awareness of students' language use, behaviours, or errors. According to Duckor and Holmberg (2023), it matters 'in a world where we grow, where we learn, and where we expect everyone to change for the better' (p. 2). These authors also point out that students need assistance to help them understand where they are going and what steps will lead them there; FA can help students achieve this by offering appropriate guidance (Duckor & Holmberg, 2023). Teachers should ask the following questions before giving feedback: (1) Should feedback be provided? (2) What feedback should be provided? (3) When should it be delivered? (4) Who should give it? and (5) How should it be given?

Five Considerations for Effective Formative Feedback

This section presents five points language teachers should consider when providing formative feedback to students.

1. *Types of formative feedback*: Different types of feedback can be considered when providing formative feedback.

    - *Performance feedback* focusses on helping students realise the correctness or appropriateness of their language use or responses to test tasks or activities.

Table 4 Teaching and assessment alignments

Purpose	Assessment activities	What to assess	Examples	Primary intended use
1. To enable students to achieve or attain the target learning objectives	*AfL & AaL* ➔ *AoL*	Linguistic knowledge, language skills, cognitive and psychological processes, other academic challenges to learning	Quizzes, exercises, homework, informal discussion, teachers' questions, diaries, and reflections	To provide feedback on performance and to adjust or develop teaching activities
2. To determine whether students have achieved or attained the learning outcomes of a course; to summarise the level of achievement or attainment	*AoL* ➔ *AfL & AaL*	Language skills or abilities related to the learning outcomes and classroom activities	Midterm and final tests, assignments, portfolios, group projects	To award a grade; to produce grade transcripts; to certify course fulfilments
3. To find out the level of readiness or	*Diagnostic assessment*	Language skills that enable success in the	Practice or mock tests; diagnostic assessment	To inform a recommendation of

preparedness (e.g., what areas of language skills/abilities need more improvement and support)	*FA (for support of learning & success) & SA (as based on identified ability criteria); see No. 6*	study of different areas of study; language skills to perform required occupational responsibilities (e.g., as a receptionist, as a secretary)	(e.g., DELNA); in-house workplace assessment	whether a given student or employee needs further specific language support
4. To admit or accept new students into a programme; to determine which applicants should be employed	*Admission or selection tests; aptitude tests; see No. 6* *SA (as based on target language constructs, skills, knowledge); FA (for test-taking preparation & score users)*	Language ability specific to a programme or degree offered in a given academic institute or provider, or to a job interview; language aptitude tests	College or university entrance examination; Test of English for International Communication (TOEIC); job interviews in the target language; language aptitude tests for military personnel selection	To accept or reject students or applicants
5. To place students or candidates into an appropriate level of a subject or area	*Placement tests*	Language skills at the point before being placed into a specific subject; a raw ability to learn new languages	English Placement Test; Oxford Placement Test; in-house placement tests	To allocate students or candidates into a programme that suits their current language ability

Table 4 (cont.)

Purpose	Assessment activities	What to assess	Examples	Primary intended use
6. To determine a level of general or specific-purpose proficiency (e.g., beginner, intermediate, advanced)	*Proficiency or specific-purpose language tests; admission tests; see Nos. 3 & 4*	General language ability free from any previous learning, specific instructions, or language courses; professional specific language ability	Academic language proficiency tests such as TOEFL and IELTS; university or college entrance examinations; specific-purpose tests such as OET; language tests for immigrants; Aviation English Test	To certify a level of proficiency; to accept or reject applicants
7. To determine the level of student learning attainment according to predetermined criteria (known as standards or benchmarks) used to guide language curriculum and assessment design	*State, province, or national assessment; see Nos. 1 & 2*	Language skills related to the expected level of attainment in a given school grade (e.g., Grades 1 to 12) defined by governments (e.g., ministry of education)	National/state curriculum standards; Bloom's taxonomy; ESL scales used in Australia; ACTFL Proficiency Guidelines; CLB standard for English as a second language; CEFR	To ensure that students meet an expected level of standards relative to their grades or levels; to promote students' self-assessment; to fund schools or educational sectors

- *Numerical feedback* (e.g., scores) is also performance feedback. It tells students the level of performance relative to the maximum score they can achieve. It is helpful to provide an average score so that students know if they are above or below the average. However, numerical feedback alone is insufficient because students may not know how to use it.
- *Corrective feedback* is complementary to numerical feedback and part of performance feedback because teachers inform students whether their language use or responses are accurate or appropriate and provide an explanation.
- *Metacognitive feedback* focusses on helping students understand cognitive processes that can help them succeed in language use or task completion. It concerns how well students process information for monitoring and planning purposes (e.g., planning and goal-setting, monitoring, remembering, recalling, analysing, and synthesising). In a writing task, students' poor knowhow may result in a lack of outlining or weak brainstorming of ideas before writing. After realising this, teachers can discuss how to improve their outlining with students.

2. *Configuration of feedback*: Formative feedback needs to be delivered in ways that would benefit the student. Formative feedback configuration is related to efficacy, effectiveness, and fairness. According to Duckor and Holmberg (2023), formative feedback can be designed for whole class, group, and individual configurations. Whole class formative feedback provides a general guidance in areas in which students perform and do not perform well. Group feedback focusses on the work of a specific group of (more or less homogenous) students, whereas individual feedback is tailored to a particular student.
3. *Explicitness of feedback*: Teachers can vary the degree of explicitness when giving feedback to students.

- *Explicit feedback* provides direct information to students on whether they are right or wrong in their responses and what the correct responses are (e.g., 'You misspelt "weather" here.').
- *Implicit feedback* offers indirect correction of students' responses but does not promptly provide the correct answer or response (e.g., 'Is "weather" spelt correctly?').
- *Recasts* are examples of implicit feedback when teachers use a proper form without explicitly correcting the student(s). For instance, in an interview task, a student says, 'I *did not had* breakfast, so I am quite hungry'; in response, the teacher says, 'Oh, you *didn't have* breakfast. Why?'.
- Other types of feedback include clarification requests and elicitation and repetition techniques (see Lyster & Ranta, 1997).

4. *Time of feedback*: This consideration is related to promptness of feedback provision.

   - *Immediate feedback* occurs when teachers provide feedback to students promptly when they realise students' errors or incorrect or inappropriate language use or responses. Immediate feedback may disrupt students' cognitive processes of language use or learning or embarrass them, so teachers must decide whether it is necessary and when it is appropriate. With automated scoring, numerical and generic feedback can be provided soon after students have submitted the work or test. A benefit of immediate feedback is that students can associate the correction with the error.
   - *Delayed feedback* can be provided after students have completed a given activity or complex language task. In some educational settings where teachers design and administer their own tests to groups of students, teachers will need time first to score or evaluate students' responses, so feedback can be delayed. Delayed feedback can be both 'holistic' and detailed – giving specific information to help students learn about their work.

5. *Feedback agencies*: Agency is concerned with the directionality of the formative feedback framework (Duckor & Holmberg, 2023). Formative feedback can be teacher-driven, but it is not always the case. Students can be encouraged to assess their own work (e.g., self-assessment) or provide feedback to one another (e.g., peer-assessment). Teachers need to support and guide students when they engage in self- and peer-assessment (e.g., how to use assessment criteria and what to look for in their work).

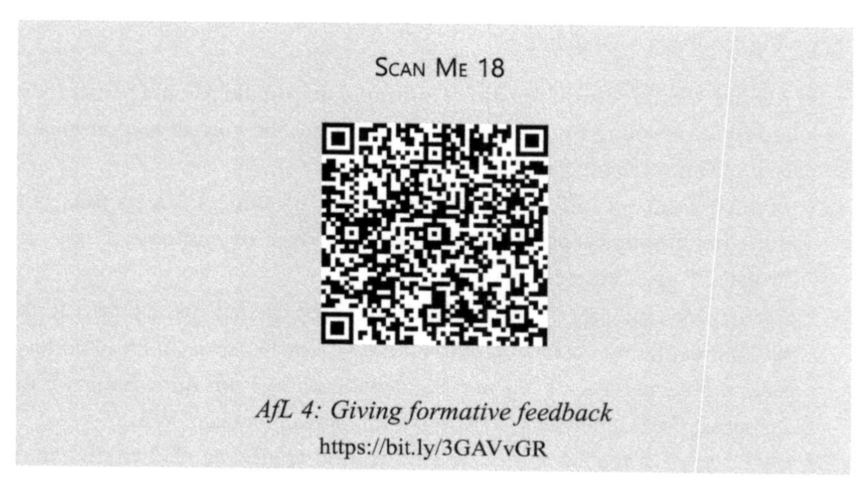

AfL 4: Giving formative feedback
https://bit.ly/3GAVvGR

8.1.3 Consolidated Guidelines for Improving Classroom Language Assessment Practices

Here, we present seven summary points that can help improve assessment practices. These summary points can serve as a starting point for evaluating assessment practice; teachers working in diverse educational settings will, of course, have to make sensitive judgements to suit their local circumstances.

1. Classroom assessment should focus primarily on student learning quality, development, and enjoyment rather than, for example, on final scores or achievement grades. Classroom assessment should promote equitable access to the learning materials and resources required to successfully perform classroom activities and subsequent assessment tasks. Therefore, the quality of learning and assessment should be understood as the extent to which students' current needs have been responded to and accommodated pedagogically.
2. Classroom assessment should recognise the context-specific nature of teaching and learning. This sociocultural perspective contrasts with the large-scale standardised SA that often separates teaching from assessment and merely focusses on certification and gatekeeping functions.
3. Classroom assessment should mainly adopt a CRA, which focusses on whether and to what extent students have met the expected learning outcomes and, if not, what further support should be provided. This should apply to both test items (questions) and non-test assessment tasks. Classroom assessment focusses primarily on the learning outcomes (within a given syllabus or curriculum) rather than on ranking students into different levels.
4. During classroom activities, time should be given to observation, evaluation, and reflection on student learning, challenges, and successes (and not just the correctness or quality of the performance, be that in the form of responses to test items or non-test assessment tasks).
5. Assessment schemes should clearly indicate how the different components contribute to the final (summative) score or grade (e.g., end-of-year exams 50 per cent, coursework portfolio 50 per cent).
6. When assessing performance, scoring or assessment rubrics should be developed and validated as far as possible (e.g., checking with knowledgeable colleagues or assessment specialists) and published to all parties involved (see Brown, 2005, 2012; Green, 2020). Without knowing scoring rubrics, students cannot set goals to address the assessment task and self-assess their performance or progress; teachers cannot show evidence of their scoring method and cannot provide effective feedback that targets improving students' weaknesses.

7. Observing and identifying classroom assessments' intended and unintended consequences is essential. Intended effects include improvement of learning, ability to use what students have learnt in real-life situations, positive attitudes towards learning, and accountability or accreditation. Unintended consequences include fatigue from too many assessment tasks, dishonesty, and a lack of peer collaboration in group assessment tasks.

8.2 Research and Enquiries in Language Assessment

A number of issues in language assessment require further research at this time. We present six issues and areas for discussion for illustrative purposes. Many of these issues cut across both FA and SA (illustrated in Figure 16).

1. Research that investigates applications of language proficiency or language competency frameworks or benchmarks that are used to inform language curriculums, policies, and language teaching and assessment across various regions around the world (e.g., ACTFL, CEFR, the ESL scales in Australia, to name but a few). Several frameworks have been influential and revised over time. Therefore, knowing whether and to what extent such frameworks

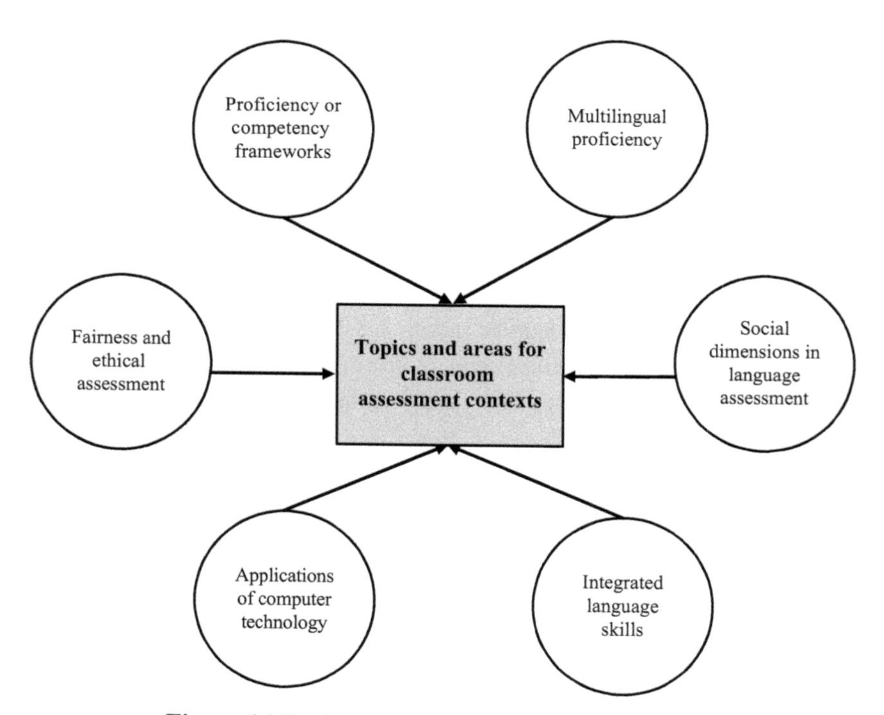

Figure 16 Topics and areas for assessment research

have impacted or been used in local, national, and international assessment contexts is essential. The benefits and drawbacks of adopting a particular language framework for teaching, learning, and assessment in localised contexts are under-researched.

2. Research that considers and explores the nature of multilingual proficiency in language assessment. Insights from this area of study can inform how language proficiency can be assessed differently across localised multilingual contexts. Multilingual assessment requires re-conceptualising the prevailing English language proficiency models, which are largely based on anglophone monolingual language proficiency theories. Multilinguals are currently assessed based on this view in many language proficiency tests. In both FA and SA, English language learning outcomes are strongly influenced by anglophone theories of language proficiency. This is evident when schools, universities, or language institutes adopt or subscribe to commercial language books from mainstream publishers that provide them with language tests or assessment tools for classroom use. There is a need to embrace and accept the presence of multilingualism in English language use, learning, and assessment. There has been a call to consider flexible multilingualism and translanguaging, which occurs when English language learner-users (who, by definition, are multilingual) use all their language resources from their multilingual repertoire to make meaning when communicating with others (Chalhoub-Deville, 2019; Jenkins & Leung, 2016; Leung, 2022b; Schissel et al., 2019).
3. Research that investigates various roles and influences of social dimensions in language learning, use, and performance. For example, SA research can explore how students co-construct their language use with others, such as interviewers or partners, as they complete communicative language tasks. What are the features of social interaction that manifest in a given type of task completion? (For further discussion, see Kramsch, 1986).
4. Research that promotes assessment of integrated language skills (multimodal language use) that reflect real-world language-use situations. Language skills are often assessed separately. There are pedagogical reasons for separating language skills (to suit learner levels and to break down the complexity of language learning). While this practice is likely to continue, it is essential to note that in real-life language use, people mix various skills simultaneously and/or asynchronously.
5. Research that reviews and evaluates applications and influences of computer technology in language assessment. The past decades have seen the popularity of Internet- or technology-based, large-scale assessments. Computer and mobile technology use for testing and assessment has become common

in FA and SA. However, teachers need to be vigilant and critical about the use of technology since its introduction changes the nature of assessment methods, language use, and ways of observing performance. Teachers should aim to examine and address the theoretical, methodological, and fairness issues and other challenges they face, for example, in test design, administration, and scoring, as well as those faced by students and teachers (e.g., test preparation, access to resources, and technology).

In addition to the use of technology for test delivery, there has been a rise in the use of in automated scoring technology (AST) in which AI and natural language processing (NLP), for example, have been adopted to replace human scoring. Developers who adopt AST as part of their test or assessment design have been challenged by critical questions about the reliability, the accuracy, and the suitability of automated scoring use (in terms of the real-world construct of writing or speaking ability). This, incidentally, has triggered public suspicion in relation to claims about the reliability and the validity of automated scoring made by researchers who are affiliated with the institutions that are developing and marketing the products.

Teachers should enquire about the use and the impact of AST on their classroom practice, particularly as there could be unforeseen or unintended consequences for students, test-takers, and stakeholders. For example, much attention has been drawn to AI technology that can threaten the integrity of assessments (e.g., it writes on behalf of students). Already, AI technology is sufficiently sophisticated that it can be challenging for AST to detect AI plagiarism. Teaching students to use AI ethically is also essential. If teachers do not have the knowledge and/or the technology to see such use, it would be challenging to determine students' actual learning attainment. Therefore, when technology has become an integral part of language assessment, it is essential to research its impacts on the validity and the trustworthiness of assessment practice and students' lifelong learning.

6. Research that focusses on fairness and ethics in language assessment. Fairness and ethical considerations in classroom language assessment are integral to the abovementioned topics and areas. Fairness and ethics are complex matters as all assessment contexts are different; each case has to be considered in its own context.

   Although there is no one-size-fits-all, bullet-proof measure to guarantee fairness in language assessment, we argue that research into practices of fair and ethical assessment would allow teachers to realise the problems that they and their students face when assessment is unfair. For example, teachers can focus on transparency of purpose in language assessment (e.g., reasons for promoting self- and peer-assessment in the classroom;

clarity in the task, the assessment instructions, and the evaluation criteria used; and how classroom assessment includes students with special needs). Teachers can also investigate how they and their students shape the classroom environment in which all students have access to equitable support and resources (e.g., through appropriate feedback provision and opportunity for students to access educational material or technology) that give them an equal chance to be successful in their learning and achievement.

We hope that teachers' enquiries into research that is relevant to language assessment practice in their contexts will help enhance their expertise and professional repertoire. Teachers can also conduct research into aspect(s) of their language assessment practice. For instance, teachers, working individually or together with colleagues, can look into the way(s) in which they design their end-of-term tests or non-test tasks, analyse student performance, and provide feedback.

8.3 Further Professional Development and Further Reading

We recognise that a high level of teacher knowledge in assessment matters is vital to professionalism. We therefore encourage teachers to join international or local professional associations that work with their members to promote good practice in language assessment (e.g., the International Language Testing Association, the European Association for Language Testing and Assessment, the Asian Association for Language Assessment, the Association of Language Testing and Assessment of Australia and New Zealand), and other local/national professional associations. Several prominent academic journals, e.g., *Language Testing*, *Language Assessment Quarterly*, *Assessing Writing*, *Language Testing in Asia*, *Language Education and Assessment*, and *Assessment in Education: Principles, Policy & Practice*, and websites maintained by professional associations provide up-to-date information on language assessment developments and research findings. Open access (free-to-use) publication of journals has made it easier in recent years for everyone to read up on research and development.

Although we have provided many citations throughout this Element, we recommend the following books for teachers to further their language assessment knowledge:

- Bachman and Damböck (2017) presents theoretical and practical concepts and issues in classroom-based assessments, such as the relative importance of decisions based on assessment (e.g., formative and summative) and assessment design;
- Fulcher and Harding (2022) is the second edition of Fulcher and Davidson (2012). It provides updated chapters from the first edition and new

chapters on issues and key considerations in language assessment research and use;
- Griffee (2012) encourages teachers to do research and providing an accessible introduction to research methods (e.g., research design and data collection) that can be useful for language assessment research;
- Jeon and In'nami (2022) is an edited volume based on a research synthesis approach. It presents four areas in which language skills have been considered, assessed, and researched, and provides an essential theoretical explanation of each language skill that can help teachers extend their theoretical repertoires for informing their teaching and assessment;
- McMillan (2013) provides comprehensive coverage of classroom assessment topics and areas, and offers articulated research questions for classroom assessment (e.g., FA, SA, quality assessment criteria) so that teachers can relate specific research questions to their localised context;
- Shohamy et al. (2017) is an edited volume that provides innovative perspectives and methodologies on critical language assessment use and practice issues. Key themes include assessing language domains (e.g., language proficiency, multilingualism, and lingual franca), assessment methods (e.g., use of technology, methods for test validation), assessment in education (e.g., dynamic assessment, washback, and test impacts), and assessment in society (e.g., test stakes, critical language testing);
- Tsagari and Banerjee (2017) presents the essential foundations of language assessment (e.g., assessment purposes, quality factors), key assessment areas (e.g., assessing language skills), contexts of assessment (e.g., assessment in educational or workplace settings), and contemporary issues in assessment (e.g., assessing young learners and students with learning and other disabilities);
- Winke and Brunfaut (2021) comprehensively treats language assessment methodology for second language acquisition research, focussing on the interface between language assessment and second language acquisition research. Topics include fundamental concepts in assessment and measurement, research instruments, measuring individual differences, and assessment of language development.

Also, the UK Association for Language Testing and Assessment (UKALTA) has published a number of briefing sheets on various topics, including AI and language assessment and flexible multilingualism. See https://ukalta.org/ukalta-reports-and-briefing-papers/.

8.4 Concluding Remarks

We must recognise the significance of language assessment in the educational enterprise. Spolsky's (2012, p. 502) metaphorical remark that 'tests, like guns, are potentially so powerful as to be commonly misused' is a moral reminder that we should all be aware of the power of assessment.

Reflection Box 7

Reflect on the symbolic use of tests and assessments as guns by Spolsky (2012). Have you seen or experienced instances in which tests or assessment practices were misused?

Share your thoughts here: https://bit.ly/48cSNTW.

Appendix: Test Specifications

There is no correct structure or framework for test specifications (see Alderson et al., 1995; Bachman & Damböck, 2017; Bachman & Palmer, 1996; Brown & Abeywickrama, 2019; Carr, 2011; Fulcher, 2010). The complexity of test specifications depends on the nature of the language constructs or skills to be tested and the resources available. Fulcher (2010), for instance, presents various specifications for the whole language assessment system (e.g., specifications for assessment production, administration, scoring, and validation). This appendix presents Davidson and Lynch's (2002) test specifications, which are useful for assessments in the classroom context.

Davidson and Lynch's (2002) Assessment Specifications

Davidson and Lynch (2002) adapted Popham's (1978, 1981) test specifications for language assessment. Their framework is applicable for an entire test and a single test section. In writing a test specification, it is useful to include the title of the specifications, version references, dates, and details of the test designers or developers. There are five interrelated components in this specification framework:

1. *The general description (GD)*: This section provides a statement of the purpose of the assessment; the rationale for assessing the target constructs, skills, or abilities; and a description of the language constructs or learning outcomes being tested (e.g., what students or test-takers need to demonstrate through the assessment tasks). The following is an example of a GD of Part 1 in a reading comprehension test:

   GD: *Students need to be able to identify the* ***main topic*** *of each paragraph in a written text. These days, students read texts on computers, tablets, and mobile phones daily. In this test, students are required to illustrate their ability to identify the main topic of each paragraph by reading a text with several paragraphs, selecting a heading for each paragraph from a list of headings, and then dragging and dropping it into the space above the relevant paragraph.*

2. *The prompt attribute (PA)*: This section describes the assessment tasks' characteristics, that is, what students or test-takers will be given to inform them of what they need to do to complete the test. A PA may include an instruction or direction to complete the task and the technique(s) to be used (e.g., multiple-choice, short answers, essay, or oral interview). The PA may vary according to the skills or language components being assessed. For example, in a reading or listening test,

the PA needs to include details of the characteristics of the text (e.g., topics, vocabulary range, lengths, text familiarity, and sources, e.g. authentic, simplified, scripted sources). For a speaking test, the PA describes how students or test-takers will be prompted to produce their speech (e.g., warm-up questions followed by a series of tasks (usually from simple to more complex ones); who will interact with them; and whether their speech will be recorded). The PA may describe the prompt's presentation mode (e.g., paper-based, computer-based, multimedia-multimode prompts) and the time allowance (e.g., 'You have 1 hour to complete this assessment.'). The following is an example of a PA:

PA: *The students will read two written passages about a holiday destination and wildlife. The students are familiar with these topics and relevant vocabulary from their coursework. They have also had exposure to passages of a similar length. The passages can be based on or adapted from online magazines or newspaper articles. The content can be modified regarding vocabulary and sentence structures to suit the students' proficiency levels. Each passage should be about* ***220–250 words long*** *and be organised into* ***six to seven short paragraphs****.*

Students will complete ***five items for each passage*** *(ten items across the two passages). They will be given* ***20 minutes*** *to complete the items for both passages. The first passage and its items will be presented on screen. After completing the first passage, students must submit their answers by clicking the 'Next' button. At that time students will be prompted to proceed to the second passage. Should the time limit of 20 minutes be reached, their answers will be saved automatically, and no further answers can be supplied at that time. Students will then be prompted to go to the next section of the test.*

Each text should appear similar to how it appeared in its original form, but this could be adjusted to suit the context of the students' learning or to make its appearance similar to that of the texts used in class. Provision should be made for students with disabilities to complete the test without undue hindrance.

Each passage will include a title and will be formatted in a similar way to the original version. A picture may be incorporated into the text if that is deemed to improve its authenticity. ***Seven plausible headings*** *describing the paragraphs' main topics will be provided at the top of the screen. A* ***space*** *or* ***box*** *will be provided above each paragraph. Students are to drag and drop one of the provided headings into each space using the computer mouse so that each heading describes the following paragraph. Each of the headings provided can* ***be used only once, and two extra headings do not*** *represent any of the paragraphs. The heading for the first paragraph may be offered to students as an example of how to respond to the task.*

3. *The response attribute (RA)*: The content of this section overlaps with that of the PA section. It includes how students or test-takers will respond to the PA. The information includes how students or test-takers should provide answers or responses to the questions or tasks. For example, test-takers choose one option per question on a computer screen in a computer-based multiple-choice test. Once an answer has been submitted, it cannot be changed. In an essay test, test-takers are asked to respond to the task by writing in a designated place and producing a specified word count (e.g., 'Write at least 200 words.'). The following is an example of an RA of the same reading test as in Point 2 (PA):

   RA: *The students will read two passages about a holiday destination and wildlife. Each passage contains several paragraphs. A list of seven plausible headings that best describes each paragraph is provided above the passage. They are to read each text first and consider the main topic discussed in each paragraph. Then they will choose one of the provided headings for each paragraph that best describes that paragraph. The first paragraph has been completed for students as an example. They are given a total of 20 minutes for this section.*

   They will use the computer mouse to drag and drop each chosen heading into the provided space/box above or next to the relevant paragraph. Each heading can be used only once.

4. *The sample item (SI)*: This section provides an example of the assessment tasks to be developed. The directions or instructions to complete the tasks should be explicit and formulated for students or test-takers to follow and for item writers to understand. Examples allow item or task writers to replicate the example tasks in parallel form. An SI may link to the specification supplement in Point (5); examples of lessons, classroom activities, exercises, or past tests or assessments that can be modelled may be included in this section.
5. *The specification supplement (SS)*: While this section is optional, its inclusion can be useful for item writers. It can function similarly to an appendix. Detailed information for each section (Points (1)–(4)) can distract the item or task writers from some crucial points. An SS may include relevant tips or suggestions for selecting topics, texts, question or task formulations, sample texts and source texts, lessons, previous tests or assessment tasks, and criteria for scoring or assessment.

Glossary of Language Assessment

Accommodations: Alterations or modifications of assessment procedures, deliveries, or administrations to allow students with special educational needs and/or disabilities to participate in language assessment activities in a way that will enable them fully to show their potential and their capabilities.

Accountability: A concept to ensure that objectives and learning outcomes are effectively and appropriately delivered, supported, and assessed in accordance with published criteria. This concept is essential for gaining public confidence.

Additional language: An increasingly adopted term to replace the notion of a second or foreign language. 'Second' or 'foreign' denotes contexts and processes of language use and language learning that are assumed to be separate and different from that of first language; for example, English is learnt and used as a foreign language in places such as Spain and South Korea. The term 'additional' offers more comprehensive coverage for the diverse language learning contexts and use in contemporary settings.

Administration: A predetermined process, usually officially sanctioned and verified by the assessment authority, that test administrators, proctors, and students must follow when completing a given assessment (e.g., instructions, order of test sections, time allowance).

Alignment: In FA, it refers to strong articulation between desired learning outcomes, teaching and learning activities and assessment. In SA, it refers to strong agreements between test construct/s, test task/s and scoring method/s.

Assessment: A broad concept that describes processes designed to collect information from students' or individuals' learning, ability, and capacity and to use the collected data to adjust or modify teaching and learning activities, including feedback on success and guidance to improve.

Assessment as Learning (AaL): Assessment as part of language learning or use. It also emphasises the responsibility of students to ensure and sustain their learning, progress, and success (e.g., through self-assessment, self-regulation, and peer-assessment).

Assessment for Learning (AfL): Assessment that aims to support and improve language learning and use and to ensure that students can meet the desired or expected learning outcomes. Generally speaking, it has been conceptualised in terms of teacher-led assessment activities in which teachers could use informal and formal assessment methods to identify students' learning status and to provide support to help them overcome specific difficulties or challenges.

Assessment of Learning (AoL): Assessment that focusses on the volume, quality and level of attainment or achievement of the learning outcomes by students. Midterm and final examinations are examples of AoL.

Authenticity: A concept that refers to real-life language use, tasks, and situations in which language assessment can be based.

Benchmarks: Learning outcomes or performance criteria used to evaluate students. Benchmarks are analogous to standards and frameworks of reference.

Bias: A feature(s) in assessment involving content, techniques, delivery formats, and specific administrations that offers an advantage to some groups of students and adversely affect other groups. The advantages and disadvantages are generally associated with knowledge of assessment content and activities, access to resources, disabilities, and cultural (un)familiarity.

Classical test theory (CTT): A testing theory that postulates that an observed test score consists of true and error scores. The true score derives from the target attribute or ability of interest that a test aims to measure. In contrast, the error score can result from specific test techniques, scoring methods, and other random factors, such as the test room temperature, lighting, or students' health.

Common European Framework of Reference (CEFR): An influential document that provides standards for classifying additional language success into three primary levels from A (Basic) to C (Advanced). They, in turn, make up six reference levels in total: A1 (Breakthrough); A2 (Waystage); B1 (Threshold); B2 (Vantage); C1 (Advanced); C2 (Mastery).

Construct: An abstract concept that is hypothesised to exist but cannot be observed directly. For example, it is believed that students must have some grammatical knowledge that informs or influences their speech.

Construct validity: The extent to which language assessment collects relevant, adequate, and appropriate information in line with the target construct.

Constructed-response techniques: Assessment techniques that allow students to create their responses to questions or tasks (e.g., an interview, pair interaction tasks, essays).

Content validity: The extent to which an assessment includes relevant and adequate questions or tasks that help elicit relevant information about the target language construct or ability of interest.

Criterion-referenced approach (CRA): A marking or grading approach that matches students' performance with a set of criteria. It does not have an interest in ranking or comparing students.

Diagnostic assessment: Assessment that aims to gather language information to identify students' strengths and weaknesses. Information can be used to determine whether further support is needed and, if so, what kind of support can be provided.

Direct method: A test method that asks students to use language directly related to the objective of assessment. For example, when students are asked to write about their weekend activities, their writing is assessed directly.

Dynamic assessment: Assessment of student performance that takes account of the nature of the task involved and the students' current capacity to accomplish the learning task. This analytic information is then used to design guidance to support student progress. As part of the assessment, students receive tailored support and guidance to direct their learning and development to the next step in acquiring the knowledge and skills in focus and becoming more independent learners.

Error of measurement: Inaccurate information about language performance derived from a technical problem in a given test or assessment task. It can be specifically related to some weaknesses of a given assessment technique (e.g., multiple-choice and short-answer questions), scoring methods (e.g., use of rating scales that are poorly constructed), and incorrect or inappropriate administration of the test or assessment task, for instance.

Error score: That part of an observed test score that is irrelevant or unrepresentative of the target language construct or ability of interest. Error scores include *systematic* (e.g., owing to a specific technique, scoring method, or administration) and *random errors* (e.g., test conditions, unexpected disruptions such as electrical blackouts, students' illness, or fatigue).

Ethics: A complex concept related to professional standards and conducts that conform to a set of collectively agreed principles regarding equity and fairness in assessment activities. Ethics are also concerned with respecting all stakeholders' cultures, values, and beliefs. Ethical concerns also cover issues related to potential unintended results of assessment activities that may endanger students' well-being or limit their future opportunities to improve their lives.

Face validity: A quality of an assessment or test associated with public acceptance and trust.

Fairness: Impartial treatment of all students regardless of their previous achievement, gender, race, nationality, culture, religion, and socio-economic status.

Formal assessment: An assessment that a given institute or officials agree to give to students or applicants as part of a decision-making process for selection and discrimination (in the technical sense of differentiation according to some performance criteria).

Formative assessment (FA): A broad assessment term to describe assessment activities that inform language teaching and learning.

Indirect method: Assessment that does not ask students to directly engage in tasks related to the target construct, such as speaking or writing, but to complete questions or tasks involving the target construct, or through one or more language use skills (not directly focussed on the target construct). For example, students may be asked to take an error detection test (e.g., Which option makes a given sentence grammatically incorrect?), and their accumulative scores are used to infer part of their writing skills. See *Direct method*.

Informal assessment: Assessment activities, often embedded in teaching, that may be spontaneous and unplanned to address students' current learning situations. It supports teaching and learning rather than deciding on students' final achievement or other purposes such as course admission. Teachers' regular use of display questions (in which they know the correct answers) during teaching (e.g., asking students to recall a grammar rule or a word meaning) is an example of informal assessment.

Integrated task: An assessment task that requires students to use more than one language skill to illustrate their ability or performance (i.e., multimodal assessment). The performance outcomes are related to productive language skills, that is, writing and speaking. For example, students read a news article about issues of animal extinction, watch a documentary about it, and then write an essay to present their position about the issues using information from the article and the documentary as well as their own views.

Language assessment literacy (LAL): Conceptual understanding and working knowledge about various kinds and purposes of language assessment, how to vary and use them to improve or inform teaching and learning, and how to use them to decide on students.

Language for specific purposes: Specific language style and specialist or technical language for a given profession or context of language use. For example, the terms 'bull' and 'bear' to describe stocks and shares market conditions in economics.

Language proficiency: General ability to understand language and use it to communicate across various language modes. Typically, language proficiency is placed along a continuum from non-user and beginner to intermediate and advanced users. See *Constructs*.

Language skill: These are conventionally labelled as listening, reading, speaking and writing. They are not entirely independent from one another in language use or learning. For instance, writing requires an ability to read, and speaking involves listening skills.

Learning-oriented assessment (LoA): Assessment that emphasises the promotion of various aspects of learning as a key goal.

Measurement: Quantification of abstract concepts or ability into numbers or scales. For example, a zero is given when students answer a question incorrectly, and one is given when they answer correctly. Their scores are accumulated to derive a total score that is then used to quantify their knowledge.

Multilingualism: The knowledge and ability to use multiple languages to communicate with others. Multilingualism does not mean equal fluency in terms of proficiency levels in the languages involved, and it may be used separately or in combination or conjunction with other languages, depending on the target audience and the specific context.

Multimodality: Using one or more language skills and other graphic/audio-visual modes to communicate or address a language task.

Norm-referenced approach (NRA): Assessment involving making a decision about students by ranking their scores or performance levels. This approach assumes that most students are average (i.e., norm), and there are extreme students below and above the average. Norm-referenced assessment is often used for selecting students, applicants, or candidates when there are limited places or positions.

Objective scoring: A scoring method that does not require personal judgements on performance (e.g., answer keys are available for scoring). It is associated with restricted-response assessment techniques such as multiple-choice, true/false, matching, and ordering questions.

Outcome-oriented assessment: Assessment that focusses on an end product, or a result of accumulated learning in a learning activity or course. It focusses on a level of achievement or attainment.

Piloting: A process of trying out a test or assessment task as if in an actual testing or assessment situation. A pilot test aims to check whether assessment tasks are suitable or work well to collect language information as intended. Questions found to be problematic are revised or improved.

Practicality: The extent to which a test or assessment is easy and feasible to use in terms of time and financial costs. A lengthy assessment is impractical because it takes a long time for students to complete and for teachers to mark.

Pragmatic competence: The ability to use and understand language discourse in a way that is sensitive to social and cultural practices in context (e.g., expressing implied meaning, indirect intention, politeness).

Process-oriented assessment: Assessment that focusses on the activities that students carry out in response to the test questions or required tasks. Process-oriented assessment considers students' thought processes, such as planning, outlining, monitoring, and evaluative procedures, and the linguistic and affective challenges they encounter during their language use or task completion.

Rater moderation: A quality control process to ensure that raters base their evaluations on the criteria (e.g., scoring rubrics) that define the target abilities or skills. This process includes collecting evidence that intra-rater reliability (scoring consistency within a given rater) and inter-rater reliability (scoring consistency between raters) are high and comparable. Rater moderation can be carried out as part of rater training and during the scoring process.

Reliability: The consistency of assessment results or scoring methods for standards-based assessment. The term reliability is often associated with CTT.

Selected-response techniques: Assessment techniques that provide students with options or choices when responding to questions or tasks (e.g., true/false and multiple-choice items).

Social dimensions: An aspect of language assessment that is inextricably linked to the social context involved. For example, in a writing task, clear instructions of what to do, and performance related to social conventions of language use expectations are social aspects (as created by test-writers) that will influence students' performance. Another social dimension of language assessment is its educational and political functions (e.g., to limit access to study at a given educational institute, to provide credentials to people who have passed a given test or assessment, to permit someone a visa or citizenship).

Stakes: A 'stake' refers to the impact or the effects that success or failure in assessment can have on the test-taker or student. 'High-stakes' is generally used to describe a situation in which an assessment outcome can significantly influence students' lives (e.g., qualified or disqualified for admission, failing a degree or certificate, and so on). 'Low-stakes' refers to an assessment that does not affect students significantly or instantly.

Standardisation: A practice of administering standards-based assessment that adheres to a stated content, predetermined procedural steps in administration, and published scoring rubrics that are applied to all students in the same manner.

Standards-based assessment: Assessment based on a set of predetermined standards, benchmarks, learning outcomes, or performance criteria that students should meet.

Subjective scoring: A scoring method in assessing performance such as writing and speaking. While attempting to be impartial, subjective scoring requires raters' judgements on performance quality. Hence, the same piece of performance may receive a different score from different raters.

Summative assessment (SA): Assessment that collects evidence of students' accumulative learning performance. It focusses on deriving a grade or final score that best describes their levels.

Test specifications: Documents or blueprints that describe and explain how an assessment or a test can be created for a given purpose and for particular students.

Testing: A predetermined procedure for collecting specific information such as language learning, skills, and ability using test or assessment tools. See *Assessment.*

Test-taking strategies: Knowhow to respond to test questions and tasks, and their awareness of how to deal with specific test techniques. For example, they can choose only one answer per question in a multiple-choice question. Similarly, in a cloze test, they need to supply one word only per gap.

Test-wiseness strategies: Students' or test-takers' know-how or shortcuts to answer a question correctly without much engagement in a given question or task. For example, in a multiple-choice reading test, students can learn to eliminate impossible answers or to guess an answer correctly without reading a given text carefully. Test-wiseness strategies can adversely affect the validity and the trustworthiness of tests and assessments.

True score: That part of an observed score that is explained or influenced by the target language construct or ability of interest. See *Error score*.

Validity: A broad quality related to the soundness of assessment design, adminstration, scroing and use. An assessment is valid to the extent that it does what it claims to do. See construct and content validity above.

Washback: Influence or impact of assessment on teaching and learning. An introduction of a high-stakes standardised test, for example, will be used to determine whether students can graduate or complete their final year and will shape how students focus on their language learning. Teachers may focus on learning activities that are similar to the test tasks or questions.

References

Abedi, J. (2014). Accommodations in the assessment of English language learners. In A. J. Kunnan (Ed.), *Companion to language assessment* (vol. III, part 9, ch. 67, pp. 1115–29). John Wiley & Sons. https://doi.org/10.1002/9781118411360.wbcla059.

Abedi, J., Zhang, Y., Rowe, S. E., & Lee, H. (2020). Examining effectiveness and validity of accommodations for English language learners in mathematics: An evidence-based computer accommodation decision system. *Educational Measurement: Issues and Practice*, *39*(4), 41–52. https://doi.org/10.1111/emip.12328.

Alderson, J. C. (2000). *Assessing reading*. Cambridge University Press.

Alderson, J. C., Clapham, C., & Wall, D. (1995). *Language test construction and evaluation*. Cambridge University Press.

Australian Curriculum, Assessment, and Reporting Authority (ACARA) (2014). *English as an additional language or dialect teacher resource: EAL/D learning progression: Foundation to Year 10*. https://bit.ly/473Z5UW.

Bachman, L. F. (1990). *Fundamental considerations in language testing*. Oxford University Press.

Bachman, L. F. (2004). *Statistical analysis for language assessment*. Cambridge University Press.

Bachman, L. F., & Damböck, B. (2017). *Language assessment for classroom teachers*. Oxford University Press.

Bachman, L. F., & Palmer, A. (1996). *Language testing in practice: Developing language assessments and justifying their use in the real world*. Oxford University Press.

Bachman, L. F., & Palmer, A. (2010). *Language assessment in practice*. Oxford University Press.

Baddeley, A., Eysenck, M. W., & Anderson, M. (2009). *Memory*. Psychology Press.

Black, P., & Wiliam, D. (1998). Assessment and classroom learning. *Assessment in Education*, *5*, 7–74. https://doi.org/10.1080/0969595980050102.

Black, P., & Wiliam, D. (2009). Developing the theory of formative assessment. *Educational Assessment, Evaluation and Accountability*, *21*(1), 5–31. https://doi.org/10.1007/s11092-008-9068-5.

Black, P., & Wiliam, D. (2018) Classroom assessment and pedagogy. *Assessment in Education: Principles, Policy & Practice*, *25*(6), 551–75. https://doi.org/10.1080/0969594X.2018.1441807.

Brown, H. D., & Abeywickrama, P. (2019). *Language assessment: Principles and classroom practice* (3rd ed.). Pearson Longman.

Brown, J. D. (2005). *Testing in language programs: A comprehensive guide to English language assessment*. McGraw-Hill.

Brown, J. D. (Ed.) (2012). *Developing, using, and analyzing rubrics in language assessment with case studies in Asian and Pacific languages*. National Foreign Language Resource Center.

Brown, J. D. (2014). Classical test reliability. In A. J. Kunnan (Ed), *Companion to language assessment* (pp. 1165–81). John Wiley & Sons. https://bit.ly/482rtYN.

Brown, J. D. (2022). Classical test theory. In G. Fulcher & L. Harding (Eds.), *Routledge handbook of language testing* (2nd ed., pp. 447–61). Routledge.

Brunfaut, T. (2022). Assessing reading. In G. Fulcher & L. Harding (Eds.), *Routledge handbook of language testing* (2nd ed., pp. 254–67). Routledge.

Cadierno, T., & Eskildsen, S. W. (Eds.) (2015). *Usage-based perspectives on second language learning*. De Gruyter.

Canale, M. (1983). On some dimensions of language proficiency. In J. Oller (Ed.), *Issues in language testing research* (pp. 333–42). Newbury House.

Canale, M., & Swain, M. (1980). Theoretical bases of communicative approaches to second language teaching and testing. *Applied Linguistics*, *1* (1), 1–47. https://doi.org/10.1093/applin/I.1.1.

Carless, D. (2007). Learning-oriented assessment: Conceptual bases and practical implications. *Innovations in Education and Teaching International*, *44* (1), 57–66. https://doi.org/10.1080/14703290601081332.

Carless, D. (2015). Exploring learning-oriented assessment processes. *Higher Education*, *69*(6), 963–76. https://doi.org/10.1007/s10734-014-9816-z.

Carr, N. (2011). *Designing and analysing language tests*. Oxford University Press.

Chalhoub-Deville, M. B. (2019). Multilingual testing constructs: Theoretical foundations. *Language Assessment Quarterly*, *16*(4–5), 472–80. https://doi.org/10.1080/15434303.2019.1671391.

Chapelle, C. A. (2021). *Argument-based validation in testing and assessment*. Sage.

Chapelle, C. A., & Lee, H. (2022). Conceptions of validity. In G. Fulcher & L. Harding (Eds.), *Routledge handbook of language testing* (2nd ed., pp. 17–31). Routledge.

Chong, S. W., & Reinders, H. (Eds.) (2023). *Innovation in learning-oriented language assessment*. Palgrave.

Coombe, C. (Ed.) (2018). *Assessment and evaluation*, vol. VIII of J. I. Liontas (Ed.) *TESOL encyclopedia of English language teaching* (pp. 4837–5334). John Wiley & Sons.

Council of Europe (2020). *Multilingual 2020: Annual Report of the Secretary General of the Council of Europe*. Council of Europe.

Davidson, F., & Lynch, B. K. (2002). *Testcraft: A teacher's guide to writing and using language test specifications*. Yale University Press.

Dolgova, N., & Tyler, A. (2019). Applications of usage-based approaches to language teaching. In X. Gao (Ed.), *Second handbook of English language teaching* (pp. 939–61). Springer. https://doi.org/10.1007/978-3-319-58542-0_49-1.

Douglas, D. (2000). *Assessing languages for specific purposes*. Cambridge University Press.

Douglas Fir Group (2016). A transdisciplinary framework for SLA in a multilingual world. *Modern Language Journal*, *100*, 19–47. https://doi.org/10.1111/modl.12301.

Duckor, B., & Holmberg, C. L. (2023). *Feedback for continuous improvement in the classroom: New perspectives, practices, and possibilities*. Corwin Press.

Elder, C., & McNamara, T. (2016). The hunt for 'indigenous criteria' in assessing communication in the physiotherapy workplace. *Language Testing*, *33*(2), 153–74. https://doi.org/10.1177/0265532215607398.

Ellis, N. C., O'Donnell, M. B., & Römer, U. (2015). Usage-based language learning. In B. MacWhinney & W. O'Grady (Eds.), *Handbook of language emergence* (pp. 163–80). John Wiley & Sons.

Field, J. (2008). *Listening in the language classroom*. Cambridge University Press.

Fulcher, G. (2010). *Practical language testing*. Hodder Education.

Fulcher, G. (2012). Assessment literacy for the language classroom. *Language Assessment Quarterly*, *9*(2), 113–32. https://doi.org/10.1080/15434303.2011.642041.

Fulcher, G. (2014). *Testing second language speaking*. Routledge.#

Fulcher, G., & Davidson, F. (Eds.) (2012). *Routledge handbook of language testing*. Routledge.

Fulcher, G., & Harding, L. (Eds.) (2022). *Routledge handbook of language testing* (2nd ed.). Routledge.

Galaczi, E., & Lim, G. S. (2022). Scoring performance tests. In G. Fulcher & L. Harding (Eds.), *Routledge handbook of language testing* (2nd ed., pp. 495–510). Routledge.

Gass, S. M., Behney, J., & Plonsky, L. (2020). *Second language acquisition: An introductory course*. Routledge.

Grabe, W. (2009). *Reading in a second language: Moving from theory to practice*. Cambridge University Press.

Green, A. (2020). *Exploring language assessment and testing: Language in action* (2nd ed.). Routledge. https://doi-org.ezproxy.library.sydney.edu.au/10.4324/9781003105794.

Griffee, D. T. (2012). *An introduction to second language research methods*. TESLEJ Publications. www.tesl-ej.org/pdf/ej60/sl_research_methods.pdf.

Hall, J. K. (2019). The contributions of conversation analysis and interactional linguistics to a usage-based understanding of language: Expanding the transdisciplinary framework. *Modern Language Journal, 103*(Supp), 80–94. http://doi.10.1111/modl.125350026-7902/19/80–94.

Halliday, M. A. K., & (revised by) Matthiessen, C. M. I. M. (2004). *An introduction to functional grammar* (3rd ed.). Hodder Arnold.

Harsch, C., & Malone, M. E. (2021). Language proficiency frameworks and scales. In P. Winke & T. Brunfalt (Eds.), *Routledge handbook of SLA and language testing* (pp. 33–44). Routledge.

Hughes, A. (2003). *Testing for language teachers* (2nd ed.). Cambridge University Press.

Hyland, K. (2016). *Teaching and researching writing* (3rd ed.). Routledge.

International Language Testing Association (ILTA). (2020). ILTA guidelines for practice in English. www.iltaonline.com/page/ILTAGuidelinesforPractice.

Isaacs, T., & Trofimovich, P. (Eds.) (2017). *Second language pronunciation assessment: Interdisciplinary perspectives*. Multilingual Matters.

James, M. (2006). Assessment, teaching and theories of learning. In J. Gardner (Ed.), *Assessment and learning* (pp. 47–60). Sage.

Jenkins, J., & Leung, C. (2016). Assessing English as a lingua franca. In E. Shohamy (Ed.), *Encyclopedia of language and education, Vol. 7: Language testing and assessment* (pp. 1–15). Springer. https://doi.org/10.1007/978-3-319-02326-7_7-1.

Jeon, E. H., & In'nami, Y. (Eds.) (2022). *Understanding L2 proficiency: Theoretical and meta-analytic investigations*. John Benjamins.

Jones, N., & Saville, N. (2016). *Learning-oriented assessment: A systemic approach*. Cambridge University Press.

Kang, O., & Ginther, A. (2018). *Assessment in second language pronunciation*. Routledge.

Kramsch, C. (1986). From language proficiency to interactional competence. *Modern Language Journal, 70*(4), 366–72. https://doi.org/10.2307/326815.

Kunnan, A. (2018). *Evaluating language assessments*. Routledge.

Lado, R. (1961). *Language testing: The construction and use of foreign language tests*. Longman.

Lam, R. (2023). E-portfolios: What we know, what we don't, and what we need to know. *RELC Journal*, *54*(1), 208–15. https://doi.org/10.1177/0033688220974102.

Larsen-Freeman, D. (1989). Pedagogical descriptions of language: Grammar. *Annual Review of Applied Linguistics*, *10*, 187–95. http://doi:10.1017/S026719050000129X.

Leung, C. (2014). Classroom-based assessment: Issues for language teacher education. In A. Kunnan (Ed.), *Companion to language assessment* (vol. III, pp. 1510–19). Wiley-Blackwell.

Leung, C. (2022a). Action-oriented plurilingual mediation: A search for fluid foundation. In D. Little & N. Figueras (Eds.), *Reflecting on the Common European Framework of Reference for Languages and its companion volume* (pp. 78–94). Multilingual Matters.

Leung, C. (2022b). Language proficiency: From description to prescription and back. *Educational Linguistics*, *1*(1), 56–81. https://doi.org/10.1515/eduling-2021-0006.

Lewkowicz, J., & Leung, C. (2021). Classroom-based assessment – Timeline. *Language Teaching*, *54*(1), 47–57. http://doi:10.1017/S0261444820000506.

Luoma, S. (2004). *Assessing speaking*. Cambridge University Press.

Lynch, B. K. (2003). *Language assessment and program evaluation*. Edinburgh University Press.

Lyster, R., & Ranta, L. (1997). Corrective feedback and learner uptake. *Studies in second language acquisition*, *19*(1), 37–66. https://doi.org/10.1017/s0272263197001034.

McMillan, J. H. (Ed.) (2013). *Sage handbook of research on classroom assessment*. Sage.

McNamara, T. (1996). *Measuring second language performance*. Longman.

McNamara, T., & Roever, C. (2006). *Language testing: The social dimension*. Blackwell.

Mirhosseini, S.-A., & De Costa, P. (Eds.) (2019). *The sociopolitics of English language testing*. Bloomsbury.

Moder, C. L., & Halleck, G. B. (2022). Designing language tests for specific purposes. In G. Fulcher & L. Harding (Eds.), *Routledge handbook of language testing* (2nd ed., pp. 81–95). Routledge.

New South Wales (NSW) Department of Education and Training. (2004). *ESL steps: ESL curriculum framework K-6*. New South Wales, Australia.

O'Sullivan, B. (2012). The assessment development process. In C. Coombe, P. Davidson, B. O'Sullivan, & S. Stoynoff (Eds.), *Cambridge guide to second language assessment* (pp. 47–58). Cambridge University Press.

Oxford, R. L. (2017). *Teaching and researching language learning strategies: Self-regulation in context* (2nd ed.). Routledge.

Pennington, M. C., & Rogerson-Revell, P. (2019). *English pronunciation teaching and research*. Palgrave Macmillan.

Phakiti, A., & Isaacs, T. (2021). Classroom assessment and validity: Psychometric and edumetric approaches. *European Journal of Applied Linguistics and TEFL, 10*(1), 3–24.

Pill, J., & Smart, C. (2021). Raters: Behavior and training. In P. Winke & T. Brunfaut (Eds.), *Routledge handbook of second language acquisition and language testing* (pp. 135–44). Routledge.

Poehner, M. E., & Infante, P. (2017). Dynamic assessment in the language classroom. In D. Tsagari & J. Banerjee (Eds.), *Handbook of second language assessment* (pp. 275–90). De Gruyter Mouton.

Popham, W. J. (1978). *Criterion-referenced measurement*. Prentice-Hall.

Popham, W. J. (1981). *Modern educational measurement*. Prentice-Hall.

Popham, W. J. (2017). *Classroom assessment: What teachers need to know* (8th ed.). Pearson.

Purpura, J. E. (1999). *Learner strategy use and performance on language tests: A structural equation modeling approach*. Cambridge University Press.

Purpura, J. E. (2004). *Assessing grammar*. Cambridge University Press.

Purpura, J. E. (2016). Second and foreign language assessment. *Modern Language Journal*, 100(Sup), 190–208. https://doi.org/10.1111/modl.12308.

Purpura, J. E. (2021). A rationale for using a scenario-based assessment to measure competency-based, situated second and foreign language proficiency. In M. Masperi, C. Cervini, & Y. Bardière (Eds.), *Évaluation des acquisitions langagières: du formatif au certificatif, mediAzioni*, 32, A54–A96. http://www.mediazioni.sitlec.unibo.it.

Read, J. (2000). *Assessing vocabulary*. Oxford University Press.

Read, J. (2015). Researching language testing and assessment. In B. Paltridge & A. Phakiti (Eds.), *Research methods in applied linguistics: A practical resource* (pp. 471–86). Bloomsbury.

Robertson, K., with Hohmann, J., & Stewart I. (2005). Dictating to one of 'us': The migration of Mrs Freer. *Macquarie Law Journal*, *5*(2), 241–75.

Rocca, L., Carlsen, C. H., & Deygers, B. (2018). *Linguistic integration of adult migrants: Requirements and learning opportunities.* Report on the 2018 Council of Europe and ALTE survey on language and knowledge of society policies for migrants. Council of Europe.

Roever, C., & Phakiti, A. (2018). *Quantitative methods for second language research: A problem solving approach*. Routledge.

Rost, M. (2016). *Teaching and researching listening* (3rd ed.). Routledge.

Savignon, S. J. (1972). *Communicative competence: An experiment in foreign language teaching*. Center for Curriculum Development.

Savignon, S. J. (1983). *Communicative competence: Theory and classroom practice*. Addison-Wesley.

Sawaki, Y. (2014). Classical test theory. In A. Kunnan (Ed.), *Companion to language assessment*. Wiley. https://doi.org/10.1002/9781118411360.wbcla097.

Sawaki, Y. (2017). Norm-referenced vs. criterion-referenced approach to assessment. In D. Tsagari & J. Banerjee (Eds.), *Handbook of second language assessment* (pp. 45–60). De Gruyter.

Schissel, J. L., Leung, C., & Chalhoub-Deville, M. (2019). The construct of multilingualism in language testing. *Language Assessment Quarterly, 16*(4–5), 373–8. https://doi.org/10.1080/15434303.2019.1680679.

Shohamy, E. (2001). *The power of tests: A critical perspective on the uses of language tests*. Pearson Education.

Shohamy, E. (2006). *Language policy: Hidden agendas and new approaches*. Routledge.

Shohamy E., Or, I. G., & May, S. (Eds.) (2017). *Language testing and assessment* (3rd ed.). Springer.

Spolsky, B. (1995). *Measured words*. Oxford University Press.

Spolsky, B. (2012). Language testing and language management. In G. Fulcher & F. Davidson (Eds.), *Routledge handbook of language testing* (pp. 495–505). Routledge.

Spolsky, B. (2017). History of language testing. In E. Shohamy, I. G. Or, & S. May (Eds.), *Language testing and assessment* (3rd ed.) (pp. 375–84). Springer.

Stobart, G. (2006). The validity of formative assessment. In J. Gardner (Ed.), *Assessment and learning* (pp. 133–46). Sage.

Taylor, L. (2009). Developing assessment literacy. *Annual Review of Applied Linguistics, 29*(1), 21–36. https://doi.org/doi:10.1017/S0267190509090035.

Tsagari, D., & Banerjee J. (Eds.) (2017). *Handbook of second language assessment*. De Gruyter Mouton.

Tsagari, D., & Cheng, L. (2017). Washback, impact, and consequences revisited. In E. Shohamy, I. G. Or, & S. May (Eds.), *Language testing and assessment* (3rd ed., pp. 359–72). Springer.

Turner, C. E., & Purpura, J. E. (2017). Learning-oriented assessment in second and foreign language classrooms. In D. Tsagari & J. Banerjee (Eds.), *Handbook of second language assessment* (pp. 255–73). De Gruyter Mouton.

Wall, D. (2012). Washback. In G. Fulcher & F. Davidson (Eds.), *Routledge handbook of language testing* (pp. 79–92). Routledge.

Weigle, S. (2002). *Assessing writing*. Cambridge University Press.

Weir, C. J. (1990). *Communicative language testing*. Prentice Hall.

Weir, C. J. (2005). *Language testing and validation: An evidence-based approach*. Palgrave Macmillan.

Winke, P., & Brunfaut, T. (Eds.) (2021). *Routledge handbook of second language acquisition and language testing*. Routledge.

Young, R. (2022). Social dimensions in language testing. In G. Fulcher & L. Harding (Eds.), *Routledge handbook of language testing* (2nd ed., pp. 63–80). Routledge.

Acknowledgements

This Element would not have been possible without support from various people. We would like to thank Jim McKinley and Heath Rose for their support during the writing of this Element. We also thank our testing and assessment colleagues, scholars past and present, and the producers of the YouTube videos included in this Element for their contributions to our knowledge about testing and assessment.

Cambridge Elements

Language Teaching

Heath Rose
University of Oxford

Heath Rose is Professor of Applied Linguistics and Deputy Director (People) of the Department of Education at the University of Oxford. At Oxford, he is the course director of the MSc in Applied Linguistics for Language Teaching. Before moving into academia, Heath worked as a language teacher in Australia and Japan in both school and university contexts. He is author of numerous books, such as *Introducing Global Englishes*, *The Japanese Writing System*, *Data Collection Research Methods in Applied Linguistics*, and *Global Englishes for Language Teaching*. Heath's research interests are firmly situated within the field of second language teaching, and includes work on Global Englishes, teaching English as an international language, and English Medium Instruction.

Jim McKinley
University College London

Jim McKinley is a Professor of Applied Linguistics and TESOL at UCL Institute of Education, where he serves as Academic Head of Learning and Teaching. His major research areas are second language writing in global contexts, the internationalisation of higher education, and the relationship between teaching and research. Jim has edited or authored numerous books, including the *Routledge Handbook of Research Methods in Applied Linguistics*, *Data Collection Research Methods in Applied Linguistics*, and *Doing Research in Applied Linguistics*. He is also an editor of the journal, *System*. Before moving into academia, Jim taught in a range of diverse contexts including the US, Australia, Japan and Uganda.

Advisory Board

About the Series

This Elements series aims to close the gap between researchers and practitioners by allying research with language teaching practices, in its exploration of research-informed teaching, and teaching-informed research. The series builds upon a rich history of pedagogical research in its exploration of new insights within the field of language teaching.

Cambridge Elements

Language Teaching

Elements in the Series

A full series listing is available at: www.cambridge.org/ELAT

Milton Keynes UK
Ingram Content Group UK Ltd.
UKHW021038200524
442968UK00016B/1279